Regional Outlook

The **Institute of Southeast Asian Studies (ISEAS)** was established as an autonomous organization in 1968. It is a regional centre dedicated to the study of socio-political, security and economic trends and developments in Southeast Asia and its wider geostrategic and economic environment. The Institute's research programmes are the Regional Economic Studies (RES, including ASEAN and APEC), Regional Strategic and Political Studies (RSPS), and Regional Social and Cultural Studies (RSCS).

ISEAS Publishing, an established academic press, has issued more than 2,000 books and journals. It is the largest scholarly publisher of research about Southeast Asia from within the region. ISEAS Publishing works with many other academic and trade publishers and distributors to disseminate important research and analyses from and about Southeast Asia to the rest of the world.

Regional Outlook

SOUTHEAST ASIA

2011–2012

ISEAS

INSTITUTE OF SOUTHEAST ASIAN STUDIES

Singapore

First published in Singapore in 2011 by
ISEAS Publishing
Institute of Southeast Asian Studies
30 Heng Mui Keng Terrace
Pasir Panjang Road
Singapore 119614

E-mail: publish@iseas.edu.sg
Website: http://bookshop.iseas.edu.sg

The responsibility for facts and opinions expressed in this publication rests exclusively with the contributors and their interpretations do not necessarily reflect the views or the policy of the Institute, or its supporters.

ISEAS Library Cataloguing-in-Publication Data

Regional outlook: Southeast Asia.
   1992–1993–
   Annual
   1. Economic forecasting—Southeast Asia—Periodicals.
   2. Southeast Asia—Politics and government—Periodicals.
   3. Southeast Asia—Economic conditions—Periodicals.
DS501 S720   1992
ISSN 0218-3056
ISBN 978-981-4311-00-7 (soft cover)
ISBN 978-981-4311-69-4 (E-book PDF)

Typeset by International Typesetters Pte Ltd
Printed in Singapore by Seng Lee Press Pte Ltd

CONTENTS

ECONOMIC OUTLOOK

PREFACE

For two decades, diplomats, security specialists, journalists, business people, professionals, and other readers, both in Southeast Asia and outside the region, have relied on ISEAS' annual *Regional Outlook: Southeast Asia*. They have come to value its timely and well-informed appraisals of the trends, figures, and developments likely to have the greatest impact in the near-term future.

While featuring a fresh new cover design, this twentieth edition of *Regional Outlook* carries on the tradition of previous editions of the book. It offers a unique resource to readers who require rigorous understanding of leading trends in Southeast Asia. Its coverage includes both insight-rich sections on the political and economic outlooks for each of the ten Association of Southeast Asian Nations (ASEAN) member states and a number of specially commissioned thematic sections. Topics treated in those thematic sections include ongoing regional initiatives on the South China Sea, the increasing integration of the Greater Mekong Sub-region with China, the implications of the inclusion of the United States in the East Asia Summit, levels of trust in state institutions among Southeast Asians, food security in Timor-Leste, the significance of second tier cities in Southeast Asia, APEC's prospects during this year and the years ahead, "smart cities" in Southeast Asia, challenges for the Malaysian economy and the New Economic Model, and the contribution of integrated resorts to the Singapore economy.

The book's sections on what lies ahead on the political front for each of the ten members of ASEAN during 2011 and 2012 highlight the importance of the consequences of recent or imminent political transitions in the Philippines, in Myanmar, and in Vietnam. They consider the very different sorts of challenges confronting the governments of Singapore and Thailand as they look towards elections in the near future. Contrasting the confusion that prevails in Malaysian politics with the stability achieved in Brunei, Cambodia, and Laos, they suggest the implications of these countries' circumstances for developments in the years just ahead. Finally, the section on Southeast Asia's largest country makes clear that trends in parliamentary rule, sub-national government, and religious affairs will have great bearing on Indonesia's immediate future. Taken together, these sections on the political outlook in the ten ASEAN member states emphasize the need for observers of Southeast Asian affairs to balance an awareness of complex domestic developments with attention to the broad regional movements highlighted in the thematic sections of this year's *Regional Outlook*.

On the economic front, Southeast Asia's rapid recovery has been aided by improvements in the external demand. Having contracted for most of 2009, exports posted a strong recovery in the first half of 2010. Direct investment and portfolio flows have also returned to the region. Stock markets have rallied, and the surge in capital inflows has caused regional currencies to appreciate; in some cases, sharply in relation to the U.S. dollar. The Southeast Asian upswing is also exerting inflationary pressures. Looking ahead, exports and economic growth in the region are likely to moderate in 2011 and 2012. Policymakers in the region, for the moment though, face the challenge of managing economies to prevent overheating in some sectors.

Regional Outlook: Southeast Asia 2011–2012 collects in one volume the forward-looking analyses of a team of knowledgeable specialists. I wish to thank each of the scholars who have contributed to this year's stimulating edition of the book. ISEAS is proud to be able to share their perspectives with a broad readership. I also wish to thank editors Michael Montesano and Lee Poh Onn for commissioning these contributions and Stephen Logan of the ISEAS Publications Unit for ensuring the timely publication of the volume. The sharp focus and original insight for which *Regional Outlook* is known owe much to contributors' willingness to draw in their analyses on their own well-informed and time-tested views. These also represent the personal views of contributors, rather than those of the governments and institutions with which they are affiliated.

K. Kesavapany
Director
Institute of Southeast Asian Studies
Singapore

8 December 2011

INTRODUCTION

To forecast even the short-term future of a region as diverse and as subject to external influences as Southeast Asia is rash. But to fail to be aware of emerging trends and likely developments in the region is scarcely less foolhardy. Equally important is attentiveness to the interaction of developments at the national and regional levels in Southeast Asia. That interaction will determine the future of the region.

In the realm of regional politics and security, no trend or development looms as large to observers looking ahead towards 2011 and 2012 as the progress of the "great game" set in motion by the increasing power and assertiveness of the People's Republic of China (PRC). This game spans all of eastern Asia. It has implications for the Indian Ocean. But it is in Southeast Asia that the PRC's growing ambitions and increasing military capabilities have begun to have the greatest consequences. States both within and outside the region have adopted a range of postures in reaction to those ambitions and capabilities. The result has been a climate of deep uncertainty about the extant regional security order.

On one level, the PRC's ever more intense interest in the region challenges the viability of ASEAN's longstanding vision of Southeast Asian security. Beijing's expansive understanding of its national interests seems difficult to reconcile with that vision, which has consistently downplayed such assertiveness in the interest of the gradual construction of a regional community.

On another level, the policies of a range of other external actors have also long shaped the regional political and security environments. American, Japanese, Australian, and, increasingly, Indian and South Korean approaches to Southeast Asia bear as much examination as do Chinese undertakings.

Nowhere have challenges to ASEAN's approach to regional security proved more apparent than in the South China Sea. While ASEAN and the PRC agreed on a Declaration of Conduct in the South China Sea in 2002, the failure in the intervening years both to implement the terms of that declaration and to arrive at a more formal and effective Code of Conduct may symbolize the obsolescence of the Association's approach to regional security. Today, it is difficult to avoid concluding that many years of easy-going inaction on the South China Sea are coming back to haunt not only those of ASEAN's member states with claims to territorial waters there but also the grouping as a whole.

American Secretary of State Hillary Clinton took advantage of the July 2010 meeting of the ASEAN Regional Forum in Hanoi to call attention to the need for a concerted, multilateral approach to countering Beijing's increasingly forceful assertions of its unilateral rights in areas of the South China Sea claimed by various of its Southeast Asian neighbours. American naval power has long underpinned ASEAN's approach to regional security. Clinton's call was thus little more than an open affirmation of the status quo that ASEAN had long favoured. But events soon made clear that a number of ASEAN member states were uncomfortable with direct American involvement in the settlement of disputes over the South China Sea.

These developments come in the context of trends with unmistakable importance to the future of the region. One is the clear sense of Indonesia's and Vietnam's rise in regional stature. This rise comes at the apparent expense of Thailand and Malaysia, two countries whose persistent domestic political difficulties and lack of clear national economic strategies have begun to have an impact on their regional standing. A second is the ever greater integration with China of those parts of Southeast Asia lying within the so-called Greater Mekong Sub-region. This integration takes the form of trade and investment, of road and rail links, and of flows of electric power and of fossil fuels. It exemplifies a third, more general trend: the remarkable dynamism that, particularly in contrast to the United States, the PRC has brought to the full range of its engagement with Southeast Asia. It remains to be seen whether Washington's rather small-bore and often symbolic initiatives in Southeast Asia since the inauguration of President Barack Obama will appreciably counter this trend.

The significance of developments and trends at the regional level notwithstanding, their role in determining the course of this "game" will depend above all on their interaction with domestic developments and trends in each of the countries of Southeast Asia. Relative to citizens of the countries of East Asia, Southeast Asians retain great trust in their governments and in state institutions. At the same time, younger and better-educated Southeast Asians demonstrate less such trust than their older, less well educated compatriots. Indications thus suggest that bonds between state and society face important tests across the region in the years just ahead.

For example, Indonesia's snowballing successes during the past decade have nevertheless left it with several serious challenges to confront. These challenges include the troubling confluence of money and power exemplified in the presidential aspirations of Golkar party chairman and tycoon Aburizal Bakrie, the continued ineffectiveness of the national parliament, questions about the quality of governance at the sub-national level, weak civilian control of the armed forces, and the alarming spectacle of increasing religious intolerance. As Indonesians again think of their country as a rising power, in terms that recall the global ambitions of their founding president, Sukarno, the need to address these challenges will only grow.

The manner in which Vietnam will address its own challenges will become clear early in 2011, with the results of the imminent National Congress of the Communist Party of Vietnam (CPV). In choosing its new General Secretary, the CPV will put the country on a path either of stability and reinforcement of the status quo or of reform and removal of some of the constraints holding the country's economy back. Should the Party opt for that latter path, the National Assembly elections due in the first half of the year will assume real significance. For they will choose the members of a body well positioned to support the cause of reform through its increasingly evident effectiveness in scrutinizing the policies of Vietnam's executive.

In a number of Indonesia's and Vietnam's important ASEAN partners and neighbours, well-established social compacts are under some pressure. Thais are due to go to the polls by the end of 2011. But a range of concerns lead many to wonder whether those polls will take place and whether their results will be respected. These concerns include the spectre of renewed political violence, popular anger over social and legal "double standards" and over the role of the courts in perpetuating those double standards, and accusations of efforts to undermine the Thai monarchy. The very modest progress of the reconciliation plan advanced by the government of Prime Minister Abhisit Vejjajiva does nothing to alleviate these concerns. In Malaysia, an unreformed United Malays National Organisation (UMNO) has struggled, even under the leadership of the impressive Prime Minister Najib Razak, to confront threats to multiracialism and the very real risk of economic decline. The weakness of its Malaysian Chinese Association and Malaysian Indian Congress coalition partners does not make UMNO's task any easier. Singapore's rising cost of living and increasing social differentiation will be the backdrop to elections due by early 2012. It remains unclear how prominently the emergence of "a new Chinese ground" in Singaporean society and such issues as immigration, housing, healthcare, and education will figure in the electoral campaign.

The Philippines and Myanmar both began political transitions in 2010. Benigno "Noynoy" Aquino III, son of the late President Corazon Cojuangco Aquino and the slain Senator Benigno "Ninoy" Aquino Jr, took office as Philippine head of state in June. The years ahead will test his and his country's ability to address the socio-economic and political problems of the Philippines' large southern island of Mindanao, endemic corruption, and the need for economic reforms. The second President Aquino benefits from an image of virtue, in marked contrast to the membership of the fractious Philippine Congress on which he will depend for the passage of legislation. Myanmar's controversial 7 November 2010 elections chose members of the upper and lower houses of its national parliament and of fourteen newly established regional and state parliaments. The Union Solidarity and Development Party, a creature of the ruling State Peace and Development Council, won majorities in all sixteen of these bodies. Following two decades of stalemate under naked military rule, the introduction of a range of new offices and institutions of government to Myanmar may bring new dynamics to the country's politics, including intra-military politics. The release of Aung San Suu Kyi from house arrest six days after Myanmar's November polls only enhances the potential for meaningful change in the country. International public opinion has come increasingly to favour serious modification of the economic sanctions imposed on Myanmar; Aung San Suu Kyi may play a leading role in hastening that development.

Cambodia's Hun Sen government continues to make a great success of deft cooptation of some of its political opponents and thoroughgoing marginalization of others. At the same time, political ties between Phnom Penh and Beijing — while perhaps not yet so intimate as those linking Bangkok and Beijing — continue to develop. The growth of those ties coincides with a rising Chinese economic profile in Cambodia. Chinese influence is also substantial in Laos, where it coexists with and perhaps complements the networks of political patronage through which the ruling Lao People's Democratic Party continues to operate. As in neighbouring Vietnam, members of Laos' National Assembly have shown signs of increasing independence in their scrutiny of the government. But the high-stakes nature of conflicts over access to resources — relating above all to dam construction and the granting of large land concessions — makes Laos' patronage politics particularly insidious. What resources are to Laos, food is to Timor-Leste, where concerns over the cost of living and the politics of rice exports have become central to national affairs. In Brunei, pressing challenges lie in the areas of human capital development and economic diversification, issues of concern to every country in Southeast Asia. In fact, in matters of governance and opposition politics, struggles over access to resources, and food security too, the region's larger countries and their smaller neighbours face many common challenges.

Economic recovery in Southeast Asia is mainly driven by resurgent exports in the various sectors, increases in domestic demand due to a better economic environment, and the firming up of labour markets and higher wages. For Brunei Darussalam, real GDP is expected to be in positive territory in 2011 and 2012. This is because of the earnings from the oil and gas sector, continuing development of Brunei's ecotourism industry, rising exports from the completed methanol plant project, and the continuing development of the Sungai Liang Industrial Park project. Since the beginning of 2010, the Cambodian economy has begun to show signs of recovery, aided by buoyant exports and tourism receipts, and sustained growth in agricultural production. The global financial crisis highlighted Cambodia's vulnerability to external shocks and the need for the country to diversify and reduce its reliance on a narrow range of commodities and export markets in order to reduce its vulnerability.

Despite a stronger direct investment outlook, consumption continues to be the backbone of the Indonesian economy for the next two years. The balance of trade should continue to be favourable to the country but exports may expand only moderately from 2011 because of fragile demand from its traditional trading partners and the strong Indonesian currency. Inflationary pressures are expected to rise further with the return of stronger demand and escalating commodity prices in the global market. In the Lao PDR, the resource sector remains the main source of growth for the country. A number of mining and hydropower projects have been carried out and have contributed to economic growth in the country. These projects are expected to contribute to growth during the forecast periods of 2011 and 2012. Challenges however remain for the country to continue to delicately manage its economy in spite of high capital inflows, managing its external debts, continuing to enforce monetary and fiscal discipline, and improving the business climate for the private sector.

In Malaysia, the current account surplus is expected to remain at a high level and to underpin its external balance fundamentals. Recovery in export demand will sustain a modest rebound in manufacturing while services and construction will benefit from the strengthening of domestic demand, especially from private consumption and investment. The services sector will not only constitute the largest part of the economy in the coming years but will also be the most dynamic in the country. For Myanmar, growth is expected to be supported by foreign investment in new gas fields and the construction of the oil and gas pipeline to China. Agriculture production remains favourable, especially rice. The rising private consumption in the years ahead will also fuel growth. Inflation is forecast to rise due to rising costs of imported goods and fuel.

As in the past, growth in domestic output in the Philippines will continue to be driven by private consumption. Current efforts under the Aquino administration to focus on social services and infrastructure will increase disposable income that will enhance private spending. Despite a slowdown in global trade in 2011, the exports of goods and services will remain an important source of growth for the country. In Singapore, economic growth for 2010 is forecast to be 15 per cent. The manufacturing sector contributed to the country's robust growth performance. In addition, the tourism sector was given a huge boost in 2010 when Singapore's two integrated resort were officially opened. GDP is projected to grow between 4.3 per cent and 5.3 per cent in 2011 and around 5 per cent in 2012.

The Thai economy is estimated to grow by 7 per cent in 2010, from a contraction of 2.2 per cent in 2009. This is attributed to the rebound in exports which account for more than 60 per cent of the Thai GDP. In 2011 and 2012, growth rates will moderate to about 4–4.5 per cent, given the slow recovery of its major trading partners. Inflation is projected to rise to 4–4.2 per cent per year due to an upward trend in the minimum wage, rising agricultural prices, and higher retail prices. One of the main engines driving Vietnam's economic growth has been its robust integration into the world economy. Looking ahead, Vietnam is expected to continue to enjoy its strategic strengths of location, political stability, and human capital to promote economic development in the country. The government is also expected to continue its efforts to improve the business environment and to provide more attractive incentives to promote foreign and domestic investment in the country.

Michael J. Montesano
Lee Poh Onn
Editors

9 December 2010

Political
Outlook

SOUTHEAST ASIA'S SECURITY AND POLITICAL OUTLOOK

Donald E. Weatherbee

During the first decade of the twenty-first century, the security managers of ASEAN's leading member nations were preoccupied with the problems posed by the rise of the People's Republic of China as a great power on the Southeast Asian stage. China's growing economic importance and political presence have been coupled to military programmes that now give China conventional force capabilities to reach all of Southeast Asia. As we enter the second decade of the century, China, assertively pressing its great-power interests, seems ready to challenge various among the fundamental elements that have underpinned ASEAN's approach to the construction of a benign regional security environment.

Among these elements, ASEAN has assumed the common interest of all regional actors in a non-threatening, stable, and peaceful region. This approach has been framed by the normative strictures of the Treaty of Amity and Cooperation in Southeast Asia (TAC), with its pledge of the non-use of force. Recent events stemming from long-standing issues of sovereignty in the South China Sea and ultimately of access to its resources, however, lead to questions about the logic behind ASEAN's assumptions about the common interest. This turn of events has given new volume to concerns voiced — pitched at different levels of alarm — that, if the Chinese challenge to ASEAN's vision is successful, it could lead to a Chinese regional paramountcy and to the subordination of Southeast Asia to the economic and political demands of the Chinese state.

ASEAN's regionalist strategy to meet the challenge has been two-pronged. The first is that of the Lilliputians: to bind the giant Gulliver that is China in a web of ties. Although no thread is alone sufficient to restrict the giant, all the threads together hopefully serve to constrain Gulliver's freedom of movement. The ASEAN states have enmeshed China in complex patterns of multilateralism in ASEAN Plus One, Plus Three, and Plus Six — this latter in the form of the East Asia Summit (EAS), now expanded to a Plus Eight. They also include China in the ASEAN-centred twenty-seven of the ASEAN Regional Forum (ARF). The China–ASEAN Free Trade Agreement (CAFTA) has helped promote China as ASEAN's leading trading partner. Although CAFTA's outcome is claimed to be win-win, China seems to be winning more.

Beneath ASEAN, but still contextually identified with it, is the welter of bilateral connections, in areas from technical cooperation agreements to strategic partnerships, forged by China with ASEAN member states. The expanding sets of formal institutional links have been given a human face by the legions of Chinese government ministers, senior officials, and bureaucrats who participate in the innumerable meetings attendant upon the burgeoning activities and exchanges of the China–ASEAN political/economic nexus. Yet there is no evidence that economic and social ties can bind China to ASEAN's vision if what China deems its "security interests" are threatened.

Premier Wen Jiabao thundered at the 2010 UN General Assembly that "when it comes to sovereignty, national unity, and territorial integrity, China will not yield or compromise". Beijing's perception of its core vital national interests is more potent in determining international behaviour than Chinese interest in claimed regional interdependencies. The example that China set by unleashing anti-Japanese demonstrations and resorting to the tools of economic warfare to get its way in the highly-charged September 2010 China–Japan confrontation over a maritime collision in the disputed Senkaku/Diaoyu islands maritime zone made this reality jarringly clear to Southeast Asia. The same kinds of issues that have inflamed Sino–Japanese relations are at the crux of Southeast Asia's South China Sea problem.

There is, of course, a second Gulliver in the region, the United States. From ASEAN's perspective, the American Gulliver has been distracted for most of the last decade by wars in Iraq and Afghanistan and by the so-called war on terror. According to most Southeast Asian political analyses, this inattention has led the United States to neglect its broader interests in the region and to fail to defend its great-power turf in the face of a rising China. Rather than tie the American Gulliver down, there has been an uncoordinated but consistent effort to stir it up. The second prong of ASEAN's regionalist strategy to meet the Chinese challenge to its vision has been to foster the deeper engagement of the United States with Southeast Asia. The effort to generate a higher U.S. regional profile has been variously described as "hedging" or "balance-of-power" politics vis-à-vis the Chinese Gulliver.

The ASEAN states have been gratified by the willingness of the Obama administration to demonstrate renewed interest in the region and to project a greater visible presence at both the regional and bilateral levels. It remains to be seen, however, whether the greater priority that the United States now assigns to Southeast Asia will prove sustained or whether the interest and importance that Washington currently accords to the region are of equal weight to those accorded by China. Underneath the publicity dazzle of Secretary of State Hillary Clinton's exultant declaration in Bangkok in July, "We're back", is the fact that "we" — the United States — did not bring any major new economic or political resources to the region. While the psychological impact of Secretary Clinton's proclamation may have been great, if not necessarily long-lasting, in programmatic terms there has been little innovation or funding even to begin to match China's economic and social footprint in Southeast Asia. The trumpeted 2010 American adherence — but without ratification — to the TAC formalized Washington's acceptance of the treaty's spirit and principles. Although symbolically important, this gesture did not alter the substance of an official American relationship to the TAC acknowledged as early as the 2005 "ASEAN–U.S. Enhanced Partnership". The instrumental value to ASEAN of the United States' new formal stance on the TAC is that it has served as a ticket of American admission to the EAS. The importance of the EAS still remains to be seen. It is doubtful that an EAS of ASEAN Plus Eight will have any greater relevance to real policymaking than its predecessor. It is likely to remain an event that occupies itself above all with diplomatic ticket-punching. What level of comity may have existed in the ASEAN Plus Six EAS may actually decline with the expansion of the EAS if the United States and China face off over specific issues. In fact that expansion may have the effect of leaving ASEAN on the sidelines as the great powers warily circle one another. It could also lead to greater Chinese disinterest in regional fora in which it does not have the principal great-power role.

American constitutional parameters and the messy politics of congressional oversight and approval mean that the American executive cannot promise ASEAN the kind of institutional undertakings that the Chinese have offered. Moreover, there is little appetite or time in Washington for having American Cabinet officers and senior officials constantly cruising through Southeast Asia, as do their Chinese counterparts. Even America's vaunted ASEAN summits have been on the margins of other events, never the main show. Neither can it be expected that American presidents will make annual appearances at the EAS. It is highly unlikely that a newly invigorated U.S.–Southeast Asia relationship will even begin to match the economic and political density or complexity of the relationship that China already enjoys with the region. Even the ideological cards that the United States holds — democracy and human rights — have lost their value in ASEAN, where China plays the trump of unconditionality. After its sham election, Myanmar will still be a diplomatic burden for ASEAN.

In October 2010, on the eve of her sixth trip to Asia in twenty-one months, Secretary of State Clinton described what she called "forward deployed" diplomacy as an active effort to sustain and strengthen American leadership in the Asia-Pacific region. In Southeast Asia, however, the political and economic fruits of "forward deployed" diplomacy do not seem great enough to counterbalance growing Chinese influence, let alone to establish a real balance of power. The operation of a balance of power assumes that, when threatened by a strong state, weaker states — if collectively unable to redress the balance — will ally with another strong state to restore the balance. Even if the Southeast Asian states had the real power capabilities to match China, they would be politically incapable of mobilizing them collectively through ASEAN. What alternative does that leave them? In her recent speech, Secretary Clinton reiterated that the United States "underwrites security" in the Asia-Pacific. This is a hardly-veiled allusion to U.S. military power that can be deployed in East Asia and thrown into the balance. The hard question is the degree to which ASEAN and its member states want to buy American security insurance if the cost is the alienation of China.

The oldest hard-power U.S. security links in Southeast Asia are traditional alliances with Thailand and the Philippines. While these arrangements are still mentioned rhetorically by American officialdom as fundamental to Southeast Asia's security, they have been degraded by the domestic political roles, corruption, and human rights abuses of the Thai and Philippine militaries. The enhanced naval access given the United States by Singapore is perhaps functionally more important than the alliances, not least in view of the role played by the U.S. Seventh Fleet in showing the American flag in Southeast Asia. A new element among Washington's Southeast Asian security links is its increasing attention to the developing security and defence relations between the United States and Indonesia and the United States and Vietnam. There is a tacit recognition that Indonesia and Vietnam are the rising powers in ASEAN. This recognition comes at a time when the Philippines and Thailand are wracked by political weakness at their centres and bled by incessant insurgent warfare in their peripheries. Over the horizon, of course, lie the full military capabilities of the United States.

Even as the United States depends on its hard-power strength for leverage, China is also building a force capability that will allow it to secure its core interest in defending its claims of sovereignty and jurisdiction in the South China Sea through surveillance, interdiction, force projection, and blockade. China has demonstrated its willingness to use force against alleged trespassers. Vietnam has been ASEAN's front-line state in the South China Sea, but China's front line is also deep in other ASEAN states' maritime zones. Even Indonesia, with no territorial claims at risk, backed off from a confrontation with an armed Chinese fisheries protection vessel well inside Indonesia's Exclusive Economic Zone on 23 June 2010. China adamantly rejects Southeast Asian protests that its extensive claims to sovereignty in the South China Sea have no legal basis. Despite wishful thinking on the part of ASEAN officials, the possibility of an ASEAN–China Code of Conduct on the South China Sea that will legally limit Chinese ambitions seems illusory. China's diplomatic expressions of support for peaceful and diplomatic solutions to disputes in the South China Sea continue to be parenthetically qualified — on our terms.

An emboldened China's bottom line has not changed. The South China Sea is just that — a China sea. China will accept no diplomatic solution that calls into question its sovereign and territorial claims. Nor will China accept a multilateral diplomatic negotiating framework involving ASEAN and China, let alone an even broader framework that might include other major maritime powers. For China, South China Sea issues are not regional issues; they are bilateral issues, between China and individual Southeast Asian states. They must be addressed in that way. China is fully aware that there is no unified ASEAN view — let alone strategy — with respect to regional security issues. The lack of a single ASEAN view in this area illustrates again the gulf in strategic perceptions between the maritime and continental ASEAN states. The maritime states are focused on the South China Sea and the Straits of Malacca and Singapore. The continental states are pushing "connectivity", in a form that suggests the emergence of what might be called "Greater Yunnan". Unresolved bilateral political and territorial disputes within ASEAN also contribute to its lack of coherency in responding to external challenges.

ASEAN's Myanmar problem relates not just to the junta's pariah standing with ASEAN's democratic partners. One of ASEAN's justifications for its "constructive engagement" with the junta has been to keep it from turning to China. But turn to China it has, with ASEAN outflanked by China's patron-client relations with ASEAN's political outlier. For the Myanmar military, relations with ASEAN are a marriage of political convenience. Those with China, however, have been a practical necessity. The August 2010 call of Chinese naval vessels at Myanmar's deep-water Thilawa port renewed suspicion that one of China's strategic goals in Myanmar is acquisition of a forward point of access to the Bay of Bengal and Indian Ocean. China's blue-water naval ambitions have been one of the spurs for the new U.S.–India Strategic Dialogue and for American eagerness to see India involved in East Asian security structures.

Senior U.S. officials travelling through the ASEAN states have emphasized vigorously that the United States has maritime security interests in the South China Sea. U.S. naval operations in the region will continue to be part of patterns of military cooperation with Southeast Asian allies and friends. The existing security-related undertakings are now linked to a new American policy intervention, through which Washington is promoting a multilateral structure for settling South China Sea disputes based on international law — the preferred approach among some of the affected ASEAN states. Going beyond that, the United States has even evinced an interest in helping to establish such a structure for conflict resolution. China has angrily rejected the American *démarche*, telling Washington in effect, "It's none of your business." More ominously for ASEAN, Beijing casts the U.S. policy in terms of a plot to contain China, with the implicit caution that you are either for us or against us. Understandable ASEAN timidity led to a watered-down ASEAN statement on peaceful settlement of maritime disputes at the conclusion of the 2nd ASEAN–U.S. Summit in September 2010. After a Chinese warning, the South China Sea was not mentioned in the statement. The official White House read-out, however, added the phrase "including the South China Sea".

The South China Sea issue has become another element in the evolving classic security dilemma between the United States and China, in which the acts of one state to increase its security lead to another state's countermeasures, in a spiraling atmosphere of heightened tension. For ASEAN, the issue exemplifies the conundrum of how to balance China by seeking greater American engagement without at the same time damaging relations with China or triggering more aggressive Chinese policies to defend its interests in Southeast Asia. What is becoming apparent is that theories of interest convergence have little explanatory value for Southeast Asia's security environment.

THE UNITED STATES IN THE EAST ASIA SUMMIT
Rodolfo C. Severino

In Indonesia in late 2011, President Barack Obama is scheduled to represent the United States at the East Asia Summit (EAS). It will mark the first time that a U.S. president has participated in this event. Driven by ASEAN, and with that body at its core, the EAS has been meeting since 2005. Its participants have included the ten ASEAN members, Australia, China, India, Japan, South Korea, and New Zealand. As talk about the need for a new regional "architecture" gathered steam in the late 2000s, both that notion and possible means of engaging the United States — and Russia — in shaping that "architecture" increasingly occupied policymakers and the commentariat.

The joint statement of the ASEAN-U.S. summit of 24 September 2010 said, according to the text released by the office of the American President's press secretary, "ASEAN welcomed the U.S. President's intention to participate in the East Asia Summit (EAS) beginning in 2011 and Secretary Clinton's attendance as a guest of the chair at the Fifth EAS meeting on October 30, 2010 in Ha Noi."

Obama's participation in the 2011 EAS will be but the most visible manifestation of American desire to invigorate its presence in East Asia and of the welcome accorded to it by most EAS countries. That desire and that welcome are, in turn, part of the intensifying competition between China and the United States in this part of the world.

Let us face it and call a spade a spade. The "great game" being played today in East Asia, if not in the world as a whole, is that between China and the United States. It is not that they are girding for battle against each other, or even for a prolonged military confrontation like that between the United States and the Soviet Union during the Cold War. It is more a rivalry or competition between a long-established political, diplomatic, economic, and military power with global interests and a rising power with vital stakes in East Asia and growing stakes in the rest of the world. At the same time, this rivalry or competition is taking place against the backdrop of — and should be viewed in the context of — interdependence between the two. This interdependence is most visibly economic, but it also involves shared diplomatic and geopolitical interests in specific issue areas.

Southeast Asia, as embodied in ASEAN, has become a principal "arena" in that regional and increasingly global contest — arena not as in venue for combat but, more metaphorically, as in site for the "great game".

Towards the close of 1978, China, the United States, and ASEAN found common cause in opposing the invasion and subsequent occupation of Cambodia by Vietnam, then perceived as a stalking horse for Soviet power and as an imminent threat to Thailand and, conceivably, the rest of Southeast Asia. Throughout the 1980s, the ASEAN foreign ministers met annually with those of China and the United States on the occasion of the United Nations General Assembly session to discuss the Vietnam-Cambodia problem. ASEAN, China, and the United States involved themselves in the search for a political settlement of that problem.

Fast-forward to the 1990s. It was probably no coincidence that Malaysia's Prime Minister Mahathir Mohamad made public his proposal for an East Asia Economic Group at a banquet in Kuala Lumpur in honour of the visiting Chinese Premier, Li Peng, in December 1990. Although shot down by opposition from some ASEAN countries, and reportedly from the United States too, the Mahathir proposal eventually morphed into the ASEAN Plus Three (including China, Japan, and South Korea) platform, initiated in 1997.

The creation of this platform took place in the midst of the Asian financial crisis, in response to which China refrained from engaging in competitive currency devaluation. South Korea was a victim of that crisis, while Japan came forward with financial support for victimized economies. Most of the rest of the world outside East Asia looked away.

In November 2000, as the financial crisis receded and ASEAN-China economic relations rapidly expanded, China's Premier Zhu Rongji made known his government's desire to conclude a free-trade agreement with ASEAN. This initiative led to an ASEAN-China framework on "comprehensive economic cooperation" and eventually to agreements on trade in goods and services and on investments. Meanwhile, China has been strengthening its links with ASEAN as a group and with its individual members, alone and in the ASEAN Plus Three context. Market forces have served increasingly to integrate the Chinese and Southeast Asian, as well as other East Asian, economies. Chinese investments in Southeast Asia have multiplied the influence of China in Southeast Asia. Physical and institutional, as well as business and cultural, connections are being rapidly built, particularly between China and mainland Southeast Asia. Only the

THE UNITED STATES IN THE EAST ASIA SUMMIT (continued)

disputes in the South China Sea and the Chinese dams on the upper reaches of the Mekong River seem to stand in the way of remarkably good overall relations between Beijing and its Southeast Asian backyard.

For its part, the United States, which has been an ASEAN Dialogue Partner since 1977, has remained a leading market for Southeast Asian exports and an important source of investments and technology. Its overwhelming military presence in Japan and South Korea and its informal military arrangements with several countries in Southeast Asia have made the United States a dominant power in East Asia. Strangely, however, and despite all these factors, the United States has had to play catch-up in its contest with China for influence in the region.

On her arrival in Bangkok on 21 July 2009, U.S. Secretary of State Hillary Clinton declared, according to an Associated Press report at the time, "The United States is back" — back, that is, in Southeast Asia. One need not share the sarcasm of some Chinese officials, who observed that the United States had never left Asia, in order to note the manifold irony in Clinton's declaration.

In any case, from Bangkok Clinton proceeded to the site of the 2009 ASEAN Regional Forum (ARF) on the resort island of Phuket, where she the next day signed the Treaty of Amity and Cooperation in Southeast Asia. That treaty commits its signatories to respect ASEAN's norms for interstate relations — the rejection of the use or threat of force, the peaceful settlement of disputes, and non-interference in the internal affairs of states. China had signed the treaty in 2003. The United States withheld its signature until, finally, the Obama administration acceded to it.

Previous American administrations had been reticent on the situation in the South China Sea. They had limited the United States to expressions of neutrality in the jurisdictional disputes and of concern over freedom of navigation and over-flight rights. In contrast, in her second appearance at the ARF, in Hanoi in July 2010, Clinton was much less reticent and much sharper in stating the U.S. position on that body of water. While generally welcomed by ASEAN states, particularly the claimants to land features and territorial waters in the South China Sea, the assertive U.S. formulation raised some concerns, including among claimants. These concerns related to that formulation's possible adverse impact on broader China-U.S. relations, to which all attach importance.

After the 30 October 2010 EAS in Hanoi, Clinton told a press conference:

This week marks the first time ever that the United States has participated in an East Asia Summit ... President Obama is looking forward to joining the East Asia Summit next year in Indonesia.

The United States is committed to engaging with the East Asia Summit over the long term, because we believe it can and should become a key forum for political and security issues in the Asia Pacific. The EAS also provides an opportunity to consult directly with leaders from across the region.

We also believe that the East Asia Summit, where you bring other countries in addition to the core ASEAN countries together to discuss political and security matters, is a very important forum for the United States to be part of. I said earlier today at the East Asia Summit meeting with the leaders that where issues of a political, economic, and security consequence are being discussed in the region, the United States wants to be there.

The United States has deep, lasting relationships in the Asia-Pacific, and we want to be a good partner, a good friend, a good neighbor. And I think one of the ways we can demonstrate that is by being an active participant in organizations like the East Asia Summit.

When President Obama attends the 2011 EAS, he will have to give satisfactory answers to two apparently minor but in fact important questions. First, will Obama's and his successors' schedules allow them to come to Southeast Asia for the EAS summit, which is invariably held in the capital of the ASEAN chair, year after year? Second, in the light of the frequent American aversion to free-trade agreements, what will happen to the Comprehensive Economic Partnership for East Asia (CEPEA) that is meant for the EAS? If the United States opted out and the other EAS participants moved ahead anyway, what would that outcome do to the CEPEA and to the image of the EAS in general?

Offsetting these concerns, of course, are the undoubted benefits of involving the U.S. President in an annual leaders' meeting managed by ASEAN and including the leaders of all the powers that count in the Asia-Pacific — China above all, but also Japan, South Korea, India, Russia, Australia, and New Zealand.

In this sense, American and Russian participation in the EAS would be good for East Asia all around, unless a miscalculation by one or more of the major powers upsets the EAS apple cart. ASEAN and other participants will have to exercise all their intelligence, realism, sophistication, and powers of persuasion to prevent such a turn of events.

THE SOUTH CHINA SEA DISPUTE: ALL HANDS ON DECK?

Ian Storey

American Secretary of State Hillary Clinton figuratively waded into the turbulent waters of the South China Sea at the ASEAN Regional Forum (ARF) in July 2010 by declaring that body of water "pivotal" to regional security and calling freedom of navigation a "national interest" of the United States. Her intervention offered yet another sign that the contentious territorial dispute over the South China Sea had worked its way back to the top of Southeast Asia's security agenda. The aim of this article is to speculate on the ways in which the events of 2010 may influence moves toward better management of the dispute during 2011–12.

Tensions over the South China Sea are cyclical. Since 2007, those tensions have been on the upswing because of rising nationalism, especially in Vietnam and China; growing competition for maritime resources such as fisheries, oil, and gas; and attempts by the various claimants to strengthen their sovereignty claims over the profusion of islets and rocks that dot the 1.2 million square miles of sea. Overall, however, it is the People's Republic of China that sets the tone for the dispute, and during the past three years Beijing has played hardball in the South China Sea. Among other things, it has bullied foreign energy corporations to suspend exploration projects in disputed waters, tightened the enforcement of its annual unilateral fishing ban, and increased the frequency — and aggressiveness — of patrols undertaken by its navy and maritime law enforcement agencies. In 2010, it was reported that senior Chinese officials had referred to the South China Sea as a "core interest", presumably putting it on par with Taiwan and Tibet. China has not clarified what it meant by this reference. The resultant lack of clarity has generated concern across the Asia Pacific. Even Malaysian Prime Minister Najib Razak, the leader of a country that plays down friction in the South China Sea, has characterized China's behaviour as "more assertive than ever before". Disappointingly, as tensions have risen, the 2002 ASEAN-China Declaration on the Conduct (DoC) of Parties in the South China Sea has singularly failed to ameliorate the problem.

Secretary Clinton's intervention at the ARF was significant in that it represented a clear attempt by the United States — and eleven other countries that also raised the issue, including the Southeast Asian disputants Malaysia, Brunei, the Philippines, and Vietnam — to push back against China's maritime assertiveness and highlight the anxiety that its actions have provoked. Beijing, which had successfully kept the dispute off the ARF agenda since that forum's inception seventeen years ago, responded angrily, labelling the airing of grievances as an "attack" on China. But now that all parties have made their positions clearer, and diplomatic temperatures have cooled down, a crucial question remains: What can claimants and stakeholders do to tamp down tensions and promote stability in the coming year?

If the political will were present, the DoC could be an important mechanism to help achieve these goals. While some analysts have described the DoC as a hospital patient on life support, the fact of the matter is that the ASEAN-China agreement is the only existing framework that can be applied to management of the dispute. Indeed, the DoC contains some potentially very useful confidence-building measures (CBMs) — such as the need to improve safety of navigation and communication at sea, i.e., putting measures in place to avoid the growing number of maritime skirmishes. If properly implemented and adhered to, these CBMs could reduce the risk of miscalculation and, *in extremis*, conflict.

The main problem is that discussions on guidelines to implement the DoC have been stymied by Beijing's insistence that ASEAN refrain from meeting as a group prior to sitting down with China to discuss modalities. Beijing's preference is to address the problem bilaterally, an approach that ASEAN member states have sensibly rejected as inequitable and as a blatant "divide and conquer" tactic. As ASEAN Chair in 2010, Vietnam made a concerted effort to move the process forward. It enjoyed a modicum of success: In April, the ASEAN-China Joint Working Group (JWG) on the DoC met for the first time since 2006. However, China, fearful that Hanoi would use its position as ASEAN Chair to rally fellow members to its cause, demurred on holding another meeting of the JWG until Hanoi had vacated the Chair. The JWG will instead meet in Kunming in December 2010. If Beijing's hope is that under the new ASEAN Chair, Indonesia, the issue will fall off the radar screen, it could be disappointed. Indonesian Foreign Minister Marty Natalegawa is on record as stating that under Indonesia's leadership, the South China Sea dispute will be a priority issue.

THE SOUTH CHINA SEA DISPUTE: ALL HANDS ON DECK? (continued)

Notwithstanding Marty's pledge, it remains unclear whether ASEAN can summon the collective political will to cajole China into moving forward with concrete implementation of the DoC. The association has found it very difficult to forge a consensus on the South China Sea, partly because it is composed of both claimant and non-claimant countries, but also because some members have close political and economic ties to the PRC. These latter members do not want to lose access to Beijing's largesse by rocking the boat on an issue that, they tell themselves, does not directly concern them. This view is a very self-interested one; instability in the South China Sea has negative repercussions for the region as a whole. For its part, China has been shameless in using its influence in certain Southeast Asian capitals to ensure that the problem is not seriously addressed at ASEAN-China confabs: Beijing is likely to repeat this tactic in 2011–12.

Moreover, in trying to persuade China to be more cooperative on the DoC, ASEAN as a group will seek to avoid antagonizing Beijing. This concern was evident in 2010. At the ARF in July some of the ASEAN states directly affected by the dispute made their positions plain. At the 2nd U.S.-ASEAN Summit in September and the inaugural ASEAN Defence Ministers Meeting Plus a month later, however, they toned down their language and only raised the South China Sea issue in very general terms so as not to enrage China further.

What is clear is that even if ASEAN and China do make progress on implementing the DoC in 2011 — and ASEAN Secretary General Surin Pitsuwan is rumoured strongly to support such an outcome by 2012, the tenth anniversary of its signing — it is highly unlikely that any meaningful progress will be made on framing the formal and binding Code of Conduct (CoC) that the DoC envisages. If, after eight years, ASEAN and China cannot reach agreement on operationalizing a set of fairly uncontroversial CBMs, what hope is there of drawing up an agreement designed to constrain the sovereignty-building activities of the more active disputants? The answer, regrettably, is none.

Progress in 2011–12 will depend in large part, of course, on the attitude that China chooses to adopt vis-à-vis its southern neighbours. In response to the comments made by the twelve countries that raised the South China Sea issue at the ARF, China responded in high dudgeon (with most of the venom directed at Vietnam). However, negative regional reaction to China's diplomatic and military muscle-flexing must surely have given Beijing cause for thought, for its truculence risks undermining the considerable goodwill that its "charm offensive" generated in the first half of the 2000s and pushing regional states closer to the United States. The ASEAN countries hope that the message transmitted at the ARF will persuade China to recalibrate its position and adopt a more conciliatory stance on the South China Sea in general, and on the DoC in particular. U.S. officials have confidently asserted that Clinton's comments "clearly [moved China] back to a more collaborative approach". Yet at the time of writing there is scant evidence to support this contention beyond boilerplate comments made by Chinese officials that they are committed to the DoC. One lesson of the recent past is that, when ASEAN closed ranks over a territorial dispute (as during the Mischief Reef crisis in 1995), Beijing switched to a more cooperative tack. But China is today much more confident on the world stage than it was in the 1990s. It possesses more credible military capabilities. And, in the run-up to the 2012 Communist Party Congress, Chinese leaders will be keen to burnish their nationalist credentials. As such, a more accommodating approach on China's part in 2011–12 is not a given.

And what role will America play? At the ARF Clinton suggested that the United States stood ready to facilitate discussions on the DoC. China is resolutely opposed to the "internationalization" of the dispute and hence to third-party mediation. Even the ASEAN member states themselves have deep misgivings about overt U.S. involvement; they worry that it might lead Beijing to walk away from the whole process. Washington has taken note of its friends' concerns. It has back-pedalled on its earlier offer: U.S. Assistant Secretary of State Kurt Campbell opined in October 2010 that he did not think it would be appropriate for the United States to "play a direct role" on the DoC and that what it really wanted was to "facilitate an environment where claimants can feel more comfortable in dialogue". In political terms this stance means that Washington expects ASEAN to take the lead with China; in strategic terms it means that the Obama administration is happy to bolster the presence of the U.S. Navy in Asia's maritime spaces and actively to help Southeast Asian navies with capacity-building support. In this context the spectacle of the nuclear-powered aircraft carrier *USS George Washington* steaming off Vietnam's coast with senior Vietnamese military officers on board last August could not have been lost on China.

While the ASEAN states broadly supported Clinton's assertion of maritime rights, they will nevertheless be intensely keen not to give the appearance of siding with America over the South China Sea, or to become embroiled in the unfolding Sino-U.S. maritime rivalry that is likely to become a permanent fixture of Asia's strategic environment. A proactive approach to the management of the South China Sea dispute will thus be a crucial test of ASEAN's ability not only to manage China's ascendance, but also to limit the fallout from what Lee Kuan Yew has called the "start of a decades-long tussle between the US and China for pre-eminence in the Pacific".

ASEAN DIVIDES
Geoff Wade

In 2010, as ASEAN celebrated the forty-third year of its existence as a regional organization, signs of its fragmentation became increasingly manifest. The ASEAN Secretariat pursued its Initiatives for ASEAN Integration, lauded "ASEAN Centrality", and dutifully held its more than 300 meetings over the course of the year. At the same time, the Greater Mekong Sub-region (GMS), under the guidance of the Asian Development Bank (ADB) and China, went from strength to strength in developing a wide array of new linkages, alliances, interactions, and interdependencies in mainland Southeast Asia. The GMS has moved steadily from "sub-region" towards "region", and we are seeing the cracks which will almost inevitably produce a permanently divided ASEAN.

The Greater Mekong Sub-region nominally comprises the CLMV (Cambodia, Laos, Myanmar, and Vietnam) countries as well as Thailand and the two Chinese provinces of Yunnan and Guangxi. However, China *in toto* is in fact a member, with technocrats from national-level Chinese agencies engaging in the various GMS initiatives. It is through this imbalance between members that a country of 1.3 billion people is drawing into its various systems the polities and economies of mainland Southeast Asia. Under the GMS Economic Cooperation Program, a multitude of new developments have been brought to mainland Southeast Asia. About US$11 billion has been injected into infrastructure investment in the GMS region over the last decade, with one-third of this funding coming from the ADB. This aid has been channelled into three so-called economic corridors — multi-country transport arteries now being built across mainland Southeast Asia. The North-South Economic Corridor connects Kunming to Bangkok, while the East-West Corridor ties the Indian Ocean coast of Myanmar with the South China Sea ports of Vietnam. The Southern Economic Corridor connects Bangkok with Phnom Penh, Ho Chi Minh City, and Vung Tau. Apart from such hardware, the GMS is also planning and implementing software initiatives in the form of trade and investment facilitation. China openly declares the GMS the most effective economic mechanism in the region.

The Mekong River, after which the grouping is named, is in itself of course a bone of contention. China has already built four dams on the upper part of the river, is currently investing in three hydropower dam projects in Laos and another one in Cambodia, and has plans for a further twelve dams on the lower part of the river. These dams will provide it with a handle to control the major lifeline of the downstream countries, despite its repeated protestations that Chinese dams have "little negative impact on the downstream water flow and environment". The effects of the existing dams are already being felt in the increasing salination of the Mekong Delta, and disrupted fisheries and reduced water supply along the riparian fringe. China's control over the agrarian economies of mainland Southeast Asia is being strengthened.

A major initiative by which this ongoing integration with mainland Southeast Asia is being pursued by China is known as the "Bridgehead Strategy", announced by PRC President Hu Jintao in July 2009. Under this initiative, Yunnan constitutes the bridgehead by which China is drawing to itself the mainland of Southeast Asia, by developing inter-national transportation routes and establishing mines, energy infrastructure, and foreign production bases. Yunnan — in both official and private capacities — is investing widely in mainland Southeast Asian states, with hundreds of new enterprises established in these countries in the last few years, particularly in the areas of hydroelectricity development, mineral exploration, and processing trade.

The related strategy on the Guangxi side is known as "One Axis, Two Wings", with the axis being the 3,500-kilometre economic corridor extending from Nanning down through Vietnam, Laos, and Thailand to the Malay Peninsula, and the wings constituted by the Pan-Beibu Gulf Economic Cooperation Zone for sea transport on the east and the Yunnan-Myanmar-Thailand corridor of the GMS on the west.

The effects of the China-ASEAN Free Trade Agreement (CAFTA) have also already been seen in greatly increased Chinese trade with and investment in the mainland Southeast Asia states. Equally interesting in these increasing interactions is China's stated aim of developing renminbi settlement in trade exchanges with countries of the GMS. In the first half of 2010, the Agricultural Bank of China started a renminbi settlement programme for cross-border trade with Yunnan, as part of China's push to internationalize its currency. Up to 50 per cent of cross-border trade is now settled in renminbi.

Funding for the economic development of mainland Southeast Asia derives from both ADB moneys and Chinese loans and investment, often difficult to distinguish. China is establishing a US$10-billion China-ASEAN Fund on Investment Cooperation to support infrastructural development in the region. Most important among the integration measures linking China with the mainland Southeast Asian states are those involving communications and transport infrastructure. An integrated railway system will connect all GMS countries by 2020, and China is providing the crucial skills and funding for this project. There will be a high-speed railway line connecting Kunming to Bangkok and extending further south to the Thai-Malaysian border. Road links are also being developed throughout the GMS, particularly connecting Myanmar and Yunnan. Yunnan is pushing forward economic Kunming-Hanoi, Kunming-Vientiane-Bangkok, and Kunming-Mandalay-Yangon economic corridors.

Other regional infrastructure projects promoted by China in mainland Southeast Asia include hydroelectric dams, power transmission lines, and energy pipelines. The Kyaukphyu-Kunming oil and gas pipeline, which will connect the Myanmar coast with Yunnan, will greatly reduce China's reliance on the Strait of Malacca. Construction of this pipeline began in June 2010 and will be completed by 2013 at a cost of US$2.54 billion.

How are the new policies of Chinese engagement with mainland Southeast Asian states and the GMS projects affecting the respective polities? How are these polities responding to the policies? The effects have been quite constant across the region, with greatly increased Chinese political engagement with these countries as well as growing military links, including joint military training. Bilateral trade between China and these countries has grown dramatically; annual growth figures of 40 or 60 per cent are not unusual. China has now become the major trading partner of the mainland Southeast Asian states.

Investment funds have also flowed into these countries from China in much greater volumes. Myanmar has seen over US$8 billion in Chinese funds invested in the country since March 2010 — US$5 billion in hydropower, US$2.15 billion in oil and gas, and US$1 billion in mining. Cambodia, Laos, and Vietnam have also seen huge investment signings during visits by senior PRC officials. Investment in Cambodia, has been particularly prominent. By July 2010, there were 360 Chinese investment projects in Cambodia, with the value of the agreements totalling US$80 billion. In November, during the visit to Cambodia of Wu Bangguo, the Chairman of China's National People's Congress, sixteen further deals totalling US$6.4 billion were signed. The funds invested are being fed into commercial and industrial development of the mainland countries, particularly in hydropower, mining, agriculture, and special economic zones. But the costs can be great. The degree to which Chinese interests are gaining control over most of the upstream industrial sectors in Vietnam is confirmed by Vietnamese ministerial estimates which claim that some 90 per cent of all engineering, procurement, and construction contracts in Vietnamese projects are being won by Chinese firms.

In addition, the movement of Chinese persons into the countries of mainland Southeast Asia has burgeoned. Unofficial Laotian estimates put the number of illegal immigrants from the north as high as 400,000 in a country of seven million people. In the cultural sphere, there has been increased education in the Chinese language in these countries, with Cambodia now claiming the best Chinese-language curricula in Southeast Asia and schools staffed with hundreds of well-qualified Chinese teachers from the PRC.

This flurry of GMS developments and the growing Chinese engagement with the countries of mainland Southeast Asia — which are in effect dividing ASEAN — have not been ignored by regional powers. Japan has been meeting with the Mekong nations of Cambodia, Laos, Myanmar, Thailand, and Vietnam, without including China. Tokyo uses these meetings to assure these nations that they have options other than China. Japan's commitments of official development assistance to the Mekong region over the coming three years total US$5.9 billion, and its government is urging Japanese firms to increase their investments in the GMS. South Korea has also loudly declared that it intends to participate actively in the development of the GMS, particularly in helping to transform transport corridors into fully fledged economic corridors and to address environmental issues. This participation will apparently be effected mainly through private-sector initiatives. The United States has hardly remained oblivious to events in mainland Southeast Asia either. In a July 2010 speech delivered in Hanoi, U.S. Secretary of State Hillary Clinton spoke of American interests in the South China Sea and noted that Washington saw its relationship with Vietnam "not only as important on its own merits, but as part of a strategy aimed at enhancing American engagement in the Asia-Pacific and in particular Southeast Asia". America's recent inclusion among the East Asian Summit countries is also partially aimed at countering perceived Chinese hegemony in mainland Southeast Asia.

The idea of "ASEAN centrality", reflecting a paramount regional role for the ASEAN bloc, emerged from the declaration on "Reinforcing ASEAN Centrality in the Evolving Regional Architecture" issued at the Hua Hin ASEAN Summit of February 2009. This concept is premised on two conditions: first, that ASEAN will develop sufficient *gravitas* to constitute a bloc of any influence or significance and, second, that the interests of its members will be sufficiently coterminous to ensure a common stand on important issues. Neither condition looks likely to be realized, much less maintained, in the near future. The first is precluded by the unwillingness of the ASEAN states to surrender any of their sovereignty to a central administration and the inability of the body to take a unified position on international issues. No influence or political centrality will emerge from a purely administrative secretariat in Jakarta. The second condition is increasingly threatened by the phenomena detailed above, whereby the mainland Southeast Asian states are being divided from the maritime members of ASEAN by new infrastructural connections, new economic interactions, and new and intimate political and military engagements with China. These countries are, together with China, forming a new bloc, one whose creation in effect divides ASEAN.

ASEAN's most recent response to this threat of division is the call for more "connectivity" among the ASEAN states. The "Master Plan on ASEAN Connectivity" was announced at the 17th ASEAN Summit in Hanoi in October 2010. It focuses on the three areas of physical, institutional, and people-to-people connectivity. But its exhortations ring somewhat hollow at a time when the connectivity agenda is already so well advanced among the GMS states. The Master Plan points to the crux of the issue when it notes, "The challenge is in ensuring that GMS and ASEAN programmes and projects mesh together very well." Explicit in this remark is the recognition that these "programmes" are in reality two separate initiatives, already producing two separate systems. The difficulties for ASEAN in trying to claw back the mainland Southeast Asian countries is recognized in the Master Plan's statement that "This is not likely to be smooth sailing, especially since the two programmes have been pursuing parallel efforts and have sunk substantial investments in certain areas of cooperation, which although they should ideally be consolidated may involve nuances and detailed issues that may be difficult to iron out."

Myanmar, Cambodia, and Laos are already virtual client states of China, and Vietnam and Thailand are economically beholden to the economic behemoth to the north. Their increasing infrastructural linkages with China, growing investment and trade ties, Mekong water dependence, and burgeoning political and military links very much diminish any likelihood that these countries will see their future lying in further integration with the maritime ASEAN states rather than with China.

The idea of an ASEAN Community coming into being by 2015 is thus increasingly unlikely. The mainland Southeast Asia states are growing distant from the maritime ASEAN states mainly as a result of the efforts of the ADB and China to develop the GMS initiatives. Together with China, these states are now forming a Greater Mekong Region, and the links being forged will override those existing and planned among ASEAN states. ASEAN is indeed dividing.

Are these changes simply a reflection of the geographic proximity of the mainland states to China, or are they a manifestation of a long tradition among Chinese states either to keep neighbouring polities separated from one other or to incorporate them within the Chinese polity? Whatever the case, we see the revival of a hierarchy on the Asian mainland, a phenomenon which some may perceive as a rejection of the relevance of the Westphalian system to Asia.

A MATTER OF TRUST:
SOUTHEAST ASIAN COUNTRIES AND STATE INSTITUTIONS
Terence Chong

Asia Barometer Data

One of the enduring questions to which the emergence of the Southeast Asian middle class has given rise concerns that class' relationship with the state and its apparatuses. The so-called "Asian miracle" of the 1990s saw the rapid expansion of the nouveaux riches in the "Asian Tigers" of Malaysia, Thailand, Indonesia, and Singapore. This expansion prompted scholars to explore this group's modes of consumption, its identity formation, and its changing relations with centralized authoritarian states. Much of this exploration was premised on qualitative studies, because of a dearth of quantitative data permitting cross-country comparison. The Asia Barometer is a small step towards remedying this analytical lopsidedness.

Jointly managed by the Research and Information Centre for Asian Studies at Tokyo University and the Institute of Asia-Pacific Studies at Waseda University, the Asia Barometer represents the largest survey in Asia, covering East, Southeast, South, and Central Asia.[1] It focuses on ordinary Asians and their relationships with family, neighbourhood, the workplace, social and political institutions, and the marketplace. The survey was conducted through face-to-face interviews, on a country-wide basis in each country covered, using standardized instruments designed around a common research framework.[2] The Asia Barometer was carried out according to country clusters from 2003 to 2009, with Southeast Asian countries surveyed in late 2005 and early 2006. The survey gauged attitudes towards governance, social virtues, the new middle class, religiosity, mass media, identity, and globalization.

This preliminary examination of the Asia Barometer's findings for Southeast Asia considers its results for the respondents from Cambodia, Indonesia, Malaysia, the Philippines, Singapore, and Thailand. These respondents were asked whether they trusted state institutions — such as the central government, the legal system, the police, and the public health and education systems — to "operate in the

---

[1] The Asia Barometer was initiated by Professor Takashi Inoguchi. More information is available at www.asiabarometer.org.
[2] There have been, thus far, a total of six surveys, conducted in 2003, 2004, 2005, 2006, 2007, and 2008, with a total respondent size of 50,000.

best interest of society".[3] Results are here considered by country, gender, age group, and education level.

Trust in Central Government

Trust in central governments remains relatively high in Southeast Asia. Four out of five respondents from Indonesia, Malaysia, Singapore, and Thailand said that they "trust a lot" or "trust to a degree" that their central governments would operate in the best interest of their society. The highest scores were from Singapore, for which 91.2 per cent of respondents registered one of these two highest trust levels. It was followed by Malaysia with 88.9 per cent, Indonesia with 80.6 per cent, Thailand with 79.1 per cent, the Philippines with 72.7 per cent, and finally Cambodia with 72 per cent. The high figures for Singapore do not come as a surprise, as other polls have shown similarly high levels of citizen trust in the Singapore Government.[4] The high scores for Thailand and Malaysia may coincide with the popular (and populist) administrations of Thaksin Shinawatra and Abdullah Badawi, respectively, both of whom enjoyed high approval ratings before their eventual replacement.

Conversely, respondents who professed the lowest levels of trust in their central government were from Cambodia, with 27.1 per cent there answering "don't really trust" or "don't trust at all". They were followed by respondents from the Philippines, at 26.8 per cent; Thailand, at 20.9 per cent; Indonesia, at 19 per cent; Malaysia, at 10.8 per cent; and finally Singapore, at 7.3 per cent.

---

[3] The findings presented in this paper are based on the data set released in July 2010 by Tokyo University. Question 29 on page 12 of the Asia Barometer English Master Questionnaire 2006 was "Please indicate to what extent you trust the following institutions to operate in the best interest of society. If you don't know what to reply or have no particular opinion, please say so." The options offered to respondents were "Trust a lot"; "Trust to a degree"; "Don't really trust"; "Don't trust at all"; "Haven't thought about it"; and "Don't know".

[4] The 2010 Edelman Trust Barometer, for example, finds that Singapore demonstrates the highest level of trust in government, at 84 per cent, among the 22 countries polled <http://www.edelman.com/trust/2010/> (accessed 25 September 2010).

A MATTER OF TRUST: SOUTHEAST ASIAN COUNTRIES AND STATE INSTITUTIONS
(continued)

Comparatively speaking, these Southeast Asian countries display high levels of trust in their central governments, with an average of 81.1 per cent of respondents reporting one of the two highest levels of trust. According to this same standard, East Asian societies like China, Hong Kong, Japan, and Taiwan show an average 58.5 per cent trust level,[5] while the global average drops further to 49 per cent.[6]

There seems to be a correlation between levels of trust and a country's stage of economic development and education level. With the exception of Singapore, societies like Hong Kong, Taiwan, and Japan, which are economically mature and enjoy better education levels, show lower levels of trust in their central governments to operate in the best interest of society. On the other hand, in countries like Cambodia, Indonesia, and the Philippines — where corruption, bureaucratic inefficiency, and nepotism are widespread — levels of trust remain relatively high.

Trust in the Legal System

Trust in the legal system is also generally high across the Southeast Asian countries. When asked if they trusted their legal system to operate in the best interest of society, Singaporeans ranked highest, with 90.9 per cent answering that they "trust a lot" or "trust to a degree" that it would. The lowest-ranked were the Cambodians, among whom 53 per cent of respondents answered "trust a lot" or "trust to a degree", while 46.3 per cent answered "don't really trust" or "don't trust at all". The corresponding figures for Malaysians were 84 per cent ("trust a lot" or "trust to a degree") and 15.6 per cent ("don't really trust" or "don't trust at all"); for Indonesians, 76.1 per cent and 22.3 per cent; for the Filipinos, 67.5 per cent and 32 per cent; and for Thais, 76.4 per cent and 23.5 per cent.

Again, these Southeast Asian countries compared well with East Asian societies. Southeast Asian respondents who answered that they "trust a lot" or "trust to a degree" their legal systems accounted for 76.6 per cent of those surveyed. Meanwhile, East Asian respondents who answered the same way amounted to 57.8 per cent.

Gender and Levels of Trust

There also appears to be some correlation between gender and levels of trust. Women are more likely to answer that they "trust a lot" or "trust to a degree" that state institutions will operate in society's interest. The percentage of women who pick these two categories is generally five to ten per cent higher than of men.

---

[5] According to the Asia Barometer, China shows the highest levels of trust, with 88.1 per cent of respondents answering "trust a lot" or "trust to a degree"; it is followed by Hong Kong with 58.8 per cent, Taiwan with 34.9 per cent, and Japan with 33.3 per cent.
[6] This figure comes from the 2010 Edelman Trust Barometer.

However, the opposite is not necessarily true. There does not seem to be a correlation between gender and levels of distrust, with both men and women equally likely to answer that they "don't really trust" or "don't trust at all" those institutions.

Age and Levels of Trust

The correlation between age group and levels of trust varies according to the state institution in question. For example, of the Southeast Asian respondents who answered that they "trust a lot" that their central governments would operate in the interest of society, 24.5 per cent were aged between 20 and 29 years old (the youngest group surveyed). However, of the respondents who answered "don't really trust", the percentage comprised of respondents between the ages of 20 and 29 years old increased to 33.2 per cent. With the exception of Singapore, youth from these Southeast Asian countries were less likely than older people to trust the central government.

For example, 25.1 per cent of Cambodians aged between 20 and 29 years old answered that they "trust a lot" their central government, while 36.8 per cent of surveyed members of the same age group answered "don't really trust". For Indonesia, the figures were 27.9 per cent and 42.2 per cent; for Malaysia, 28.6 per cent and 37.9 per cent; for the Philippines, 13.8 per cent and 31.6 per cent; for Singapore, 20.9 per cent and 16.5 per cent; and for Thailand, 21.9 per cent and 27.2 per cent. Youth in the Philippines had the least amount of trust in their central government. Any correlation between age and levels of trust in other institutions, like the public health or education system, is less obvious.

This correlation between age levels and levels of trust in central governments is as strong in East Asian and in Southeast Asian societies. With the exception of Japan, young respondents from China, Hong Kong and Taiwan were much more likely to distrust their central governments. In China, 21.5 per cent of respondents aged between 20 and 29 years old answered "trusted a lot", while 25.5 per cent answered "don't really trust"; 6.1 per cent of Hong Kong respondents in the same age group answered "trust a lot", while 26.1 per cent answered "don't really trust"; while 8.3 per cent of respondents on Taiwan answered "trusted a lot", with 29.5 per cent answering "don't really trust". Only Japan saw a different pattern; 18.2 per cent in this age group replied "trust a lot", with the figure falling to 16.4 per cent for those who answered "don't really trust".

Another clear correlation between age and trust can be found when young citizens were asked about the police. Here citizens aged between 20 and 29 years old in all Southeast Asian countries were more likely to express higher levels of distrust. Among young Cambodians, 33.3 per cent answered that they "trust a lot" that the police will operate in the best interest of their society, while 34.9 per cent answered "don't really trust". The corresponding figures for young Indonesians were 29.5 per cent ("trust a lot") and 37.7 per cent ("don't really trust"); for young Malaysians, 28.3 per cent and 35.7 per cent; for young Filipinos, 23.3 per cent and 30.2 per cent; for young Singaporeans, 20.4 per cent and 26.2 per cent; and, finally, for young Thais, 25.2 per cent and 28.9 per cent, respectively. The noteworthy finding here is that young Singaporeans were, like their Southeast Asian counterparts, more likely to say that they "don't really trust" the police than that they "trust a lot".

Education and Levels of Trust

Finally, and perhaps most pertinent to any effort better to understand the region's middle class, comes the correlation between respondents' education levels and their trust in state institutions. Respondents were divided into three different education levels — "low", "mid", and "high".[7] In general, the trend appears to be that respondents with "low" education levels are more likely to trust their central governments while those with mid-high levels of education are less likely to do so. For example, of the respondents across the region who purported to "trust a lot" in the central government to operate in society's interest, 51 per cent had "low" education levels. However, of those who answered "don't really trust", 54 per cent enjoyed "mid-high" levels of education as opposed to 46 per cent who had "low" levels of education. More starkly, the percentage of "mid-high" education respondents who answered "don't trust at all" was 64.6 per cent, meaning that a clear majority among better-educated Southeast Asian respondents was less likely to trust their governments.

Paradoxically, too, those who showed the highest level of trust in their public education systems were those who had "low" levels of education. Respondents with "mid-high"-level educations were more likely to have lower levels of trust in their public education system.

Conclusions

The Asia Barometer data set is broad-based and notable for its large sample size. There are, however, many limitations to it. For example, it fails to offer clear definitions of concepts like "trust" or to account for the different ways in which such concepts may be interpreted by respondents from different cultures. It also lacks a clear quantifiable cross-country scale of analysis, whereby terms like "low", "mid", and "high" education would mean exactly the same thing in Singapore and in Cambodia. Nevertheless, the data set offers a broad sketch of the values and perceptions of Southeast Asians as they relate to a variety of issues.

From the data set and findings presented above, three general conclusions may be drawn. First, the level of trust in central governments and state institutions remains relatively high in Southeast Asia, compared to East Asia and the rest of the world. Second, younger Southeast Asians tend to be less trusting of their governments and state institutions than their older counterparts. Third, those who enjoy better education tend to be less trusting of the public education system and other state institutions.

[7] The data set does not make clear what constitutes a "low", "mid", or "high" level of education.

TIMOR-LESTE: FOOD SECURITY AND PROFITS

Douglas Kammen

In a region long renowned for rice production, the ASEAN countries now include the world's two largest rice exporters, Thailand and Vietnam; the world's largest rice importer, the Philippines; and two micro-states wholly dependent on imported rice, Singapore and Brunei. Beyond the ASEAN-10, but very close by, newly independent Timor-Leste has emerged as another major importer of rice. In relative terms, it is indeed now even more dependent on rice imports than the Philippines. Official policy in Dili prioritizes domestic food self-sufficiency. Yet in the eight years since the restoration of Timor-Leste's independence rice imports have become a hotly debated issue and a central instrument of state policy, serving the populist political interests of the Parliamentary Majority Alliance (AMP) government and the private interests of those in power. Global weather predictions and rapidly rising grain prices mean that food security looms as a major threat to Timor-Leste in the coming year.

The island of Timor has historically faced food deficits, and the population on both sides of the border separating Indonesian West Timor and Timor-Leste refer to the annual period of shortages as the "hungry season". Under Portuguese rule, little was done to increase food production in the eastern half of the island. The colonial regime relied on imported rice to feed the civil service and the military. Following the Indonesian invasion of East Timor in 1975, the massive displacement of the population — first in flight to the mountains, later downward into forced resettlement camps — crippled agricultural production and resulted in a massive famine between 1979 and 1981. Beginning in the early 1980s, the occupying regime made large investments in agriculture. It brought extensive tracts under paddy production, built irrigation works, and introduced new seed varieties, mechanization, and the use of fertilizers. While rice deficits persisted, output grew steadily through the 1990s, reaching a mid-decade peak of 59,000 metric tons of milled rice. Deficits were offset by the state logistics board, which imported rice from Indonesia and set market prices.

At the time of Timor-Leste's independence in May 2002, the new government released an ambitious National Development Plan, which included calls for agricultural self-sufficiency. Despite this policy, little was done to support the agricultural sector. Between 2002 and 2005 the country relied on private-sector imports of roughly 40,000 metric tons of rice per year. The 2006 political crisis resulted in the internal displacement of more than 100,000 people into makeshift camps and in economic paralysis. In response, the Dili government and international organizations launched efforts to provide humanitarian assistance, fueling a sharp increase in rice imports. In addition, government contracts and distribution mechanisms became the subject of accusations of political manipulation, and as rice disappeared from the market in early 2007 angry citizens looted warehouses

TIMOR-LESTE: FOOD SECURITY AND PROFITS (continued)

in the capital. Food security had become intertwined with peacekeeping and the quest for political stability in Timor-Leste.

Before it came to power under the leadership of Prime Minister Xanana Gusmão in August 2007, the AMP had campaigned on a platform of resolving armed conflict, emptying the camps holding internally displaced persons, and stabilizing the economy. The provision of food was central to each of these objectives. State budget allocations for rice procurement soared: they reached US$56 million in 2008, US$38 million in 2009, and, following mid-year budget revisions, US$42 million in 2010. Eager to stimulate the private sector, the AMP government granted contracts to Timorese business people to import rice on behalf of the government. These contracts were granted to political cronies, including the wife of the Minister of Economic Development and a company in which the Prime Minister's daughter owned shares. Profits from these contracts have ranged between 20 and 25 per cent of their total value. These profit rates on rice imports have enabled members of Timor-Leste's political elite to enrich themselves. They have also provided a convenient means of buying off members of the opposition and other political constituencies. In August 2010, for example, the most recent round of contracts were granted to sixty-eight veterans of the armed struggle for independence, and the Minister of Tourism, Commerce and Industry alone stands to pocket approximately US$2 million in personal profits.

Rice imports have also come to serve populist political needs. The government has subsidized the price of imported rice sold to the public. But distribution mechanisms have been fraught with problems and characterized by extensive profiteering. The rice subsidy most benefits urban dwellers. It has done the least for those living in rural areas. For example, rice in the capital is sold at 25 per cent above the specified price while that in the southern districts sells at 50 per cent above the government price. More worrying still, subsidized white rice from Vietnam is now at least 50 per cent cheaper than domestically produced rice, undermining efforts to increase domestic production. Estimates of domestic food production vary widely. The Ministry of Agriculture has reported huge increases in production (79,000 metric tons in 2009) and calculates that the country only needs to import 31,000 metric tons. These figures are contradicted by the large quantities of rice (80,000 metric tons) imported through the private sector by the Ministry of Tourism, Commerce and Industry.

The political uses of rice and rice contracts in Timor-Leste have come under increasing scrutiny. In 2010 a parliamentary commission investigated accusations of nepotism in the granting of contracts, charges that importers had not imported the quantities specified in contracts, and corruption. The commission's report, however, has not been released, and the AMP-dominated Parliament now claims that the time within which the report can be discussed has elapsed. Without full transparency concerning domestic food production and government contracts and without proper mechanisms for the distribution of subsidized rice, food security will remain a focus of political debate.

Meteorological and market predictions for the coming months make food security in Timor-Leste a particularly grave matter today. La Niña conditions have led to predictions that the 2010–11 rainy season will be the worst in recorded history. Massive floods in the southern part of Timor-Leste destroyed some of the best rice land in mid-2010, and unusually wet weather on the north coast is threatening the current harvest. The combination of fires in Russia and floods in Pakistan and elsewhere is driving global grain prices up, and some analysts are suggesting that rice prices in early 2010 may exceed the US$1,100 per metric ton reached in 2008. Reduced domestic production and soaring global grain prices will put new pressures on the state budget and necessitate new mechanisms to ensure that the population has access to food. At the same time, the country's current rice import levels are not sustainable. They do, however, provide opportunities for the government to use rice subsidies as a centrepiece of populist policies, to use rice contracts to win over key constituencies, and for members of the national elite to seek personal profit.

Timor-Leste's dependence on imported rice and vulnerability to international market volatility provides an important reminder for the region as a whole. Regional efforts to ensure food security have been weak. Neither the ASEAN Emergency Rice Reserve, established in 1979, nor the ASEAN Plus Three Emergency Rice Reserve, initiated in 2003, holds sufficient quantities of rice or has developed the distribution mechanisms necessary to address sharp price fluctuations or local disasters. Furthermore, despite efforts to promote trade liberalization, at the peak of the 2008 international rice crisis Thailand proposed the creation of a rice cartel. While the proposal was dropped, there is every reason to think that the current (2010–11) increase in rice prices will again raise tensions between rice importing and exporting nations in the region.

THE ASEAN-10

Brunei Darussalam

Pushpa Thambipillai

Political, economic, and sociocultural measures adopted each year bring Brunei Darussalam closer to the long-term goal embodied in the Wawasan (Vision) 2035: to turn Brunei into a developed country, one that is well regarded internationally. Brunei is at the mid-point of its first five-year development plan (2007–12) under the Wawasan. It continues to implement policies to reach its targets for education and human resource development, economic and business development, institutional and infrastructure development, and environmental protection and national security. Two issue areas that will continue to be in focus during the next two to three years will be food security, especially through an effort to increase rice production, and energy security, including conservation of existing supplies and the search for new sources of energy.

Domestically, there are no major concerns in governance or administration. Brunei's head of state and of government, Sultan Haji Hassanal Bolkiah, has ensured that the appointees in place at the head of the various state institutions will work toward fulfilling expected responsibilities. The Sultan himself also heads the Ministries of Defence and Finance, and holds the top positions in the armed forces and police. Crown Prince Al-Muhtadee Billah, the second most important person in the political hierarchy and future head of state and government, is now well established in his roles as Senior Minister, a general in the Royal Brunei Armed Forces, and as Deputy Inspector General of Police.

BRUNEI DARUSSALAM

Land Area:	5,770 sq. km.
Population (2009 World Bank data):	399,687
Capital:	Bandar Seri Begawan
Type of Government:	Monarchy
Head of State and Government:	Sultan Haji Hassanal Bolkiah Muizzaddin Waddaulah
Currency Used:	Brunei dollar
US$ Exchange Rate (2 December 2010):	US$1 = B$1.31

The Council of Cabinet ranks as another important state institution. A reshuffle of the ministers took place in June 2010; the new members will serve for the next five years. There will be no major policy shift, as the majority in the cabinet constitute familiar faces. However, the median age of the cabinet has been lowered with the retirement of some senior ministers, notably from the Ministries of Education and Religious Affairs, as well as the promotion of a few deputy ministers to full minister and the inclusion of younger deputy ministers. The appointment of the first woman to the cabinet — to the post of Deputy Minister of Culture, Youth and Sports — has given prominence to women's participation at the highest level. Two other leading women, serving as ambassador-at-large and attorney general, also hold ministerial rank. Their prominence signifies the increasingly important role of Brunei's women generally, a number of whom now hold high-ranking positions in this moderate Malay Muslim monarchy.

The appointed unicameral legislature, which includes cabinet members, titled persons, and district and village-level representatives, is likely to continue to operate in its current fashion until such a time when elections are held to choose part of the legislature — specifically the district and village representatives. Its annual session has offered the opportunity for the government publicly to explain the national budget, and for each cabinet minister to explain his respective ministry's policies and financial commitments. The ministers also come under scrutiny as they respond to questions from the "back benchers" in the legislature. There are no signs of imminent changes to these arrangements, though previous statements did engender some expectation of elections. There is no indication of grass-roots demand for changes to the political status quo. Brunei's unique legislative arrangements have not prevented members of the assembly from being part of the ASEAN Inter-Parliamentary Association, the non-governmental organization made up of elected representatives from the various member states' legislatures. However, it should be stressed that the legislature in Brunei is not empowered to enact laws, but merely to debate and discuss policy issues. In this hereditary monarchy, the executive — the Sultan — in consultation with the cabinet is the source of legal provisions for the state. This arrangement is likely to persist into the foreseeable future.

The Sultan will also continue to exercise his multiple roles. Through his frequent *titah* (official speeches), he reviews the progress in selected policy areas and demands explanations for states of affairs that he deems unsatisfactory. Similarly, he undertakes regular visits to government departments to experience at first hand the quality of services rendered to the public.

The major long-term strategy for Brunei's leadership will continue to focus on maintaining the country's high per capita income of some US$30,000, depending on the global price of oil, and the social-welfare benefits that its population has come to expect from the state. In part, the population has become overly reliant on the government for free services like education and health and for employment opportunities. The emphasis of the national strategy is continuing to meet popular expectations in the context of a national income dependent on non-renewable natural resources. Exploration for new hydrocarbon wells continues offshore and onshore, as the known reserves have already dwindled to an expected life-span of twenty years. Fortunately, new explorations appear promising; they thus augur well for the future well-being of the state and the people. In its concern for energy security and for the promotion of exploration, conservation, and the search for alternatives to hydrocarbon sources, Brunei's hydrocarbon sector has widened its range of business partners. It has allowed interested parties other than the sector's dominant player, the Brunei Shell Petroleum Company, to participate in the oil and gas sector.

In its emphasis on food security, the national strategy is focused above all on rice production and the means to increase the quantity and quality of locally grown rice. Local consumer preferences are for high-quality rice. Increasing the country's level of self-sufficiency in rice from 10 to 60 per cent will prove a tall order. Nevertheless, Brunei hopes to achieve this goal in the next decade or so. Various rice experts, including those from China, South Korea, the Philippines, and Singapore, have been engaged to assist Brunei in the realization of this ambitious long-term goal.

Diversification of the economy will serve the twin strategies of seeking new sources of income and creating new areas of employment to provide the foundation for domestic political stability in a period during which opportunities in the public sector do not keep pace with the youthful population's rising demand for jobs. The constant emphasis on economic security and on the importance of human capital development, of the promotion of small businesses, of seeking niche markets in areas like halal products and in agro industry, and of undertaking a number of mega-projects with the help of foreign investment reflect these goals. Several hurdles need to be overcome: improving the efficiency of those parts of the bureaucracy responsible for "doing business in Brunei", attracting foreign investors, and judiciously promoting local products and enterprises abroad. Self-criticism, as evident in public speeches, has now become acceptable. The public sector takes a positive attitude towards improving the business environment, which generally ranks poorly when compared to those of neighbouring states. Brunei still needs to undertake a great deal of improvement in order to make itself attractive enough for the private sector to play a more independent and significant role. That sector must do more than merely depend on public-sector activities like the development of infrastructure. Small-business entrepreneurs are emerging and ought to grow more visible in the next few years if they can make use of several currently available but under-utilized support schemes.

Ensuring that the next generation of Bruneians will live in as peaceful and stable an environment as the country's citizens now enjoy is the long-term goal. It accounts for the emphasis on universal education, good health care, and opportunities to excel in the foundation that the current generation of Brunei's leadership seeks to lay. Despite positive intentions, cracks have begun to appear in the society, in the form of petty crime, drug use, the work of local drug mules for foreign operators, local involvement in smuggling drugs into Brunei, illegal immigration, and the smuggling of contraband items for a quick profit. Despite the active role of the Anti-Narcotics Bureau, reported drug-related crimes seem to be increasing. As a result, several national agencies, including the Anti-Corruption Agency, have sought to promote good moral values and to disseminate positive messages among the young, including among primary school children. Religious education and practice will remain the most important social tool to inculcate the desired goals of the country.

The nature of Brunei's economic dependence and the political-security interests associated with small-state vulnerability mean that it will continue to be externally oriented. The country has, however, shown its ability to be independent in its foreign policy outlook. It has engaged with bilateral partners that it considers long-term allies, like the United Kingdom, the United States, Malaysia, and Singapore, while regarding its regional membership in ASEAN as a significant aspect of its foreign relations. It confidently awaits its turn at the ASEAN chairmanship in 2013 (originally due in 2011, swapped with Indonesia on the latter's request). It will also pursue its national interests beyond the ASEAN framework, through the Organization of the Islamic Conference, the newly established Trans-Pacific Partnership, and other multilateral fora that it considers significant. There appears to be no imminent threat to the state or the political system, but Brunei is nevertheless upgrading its external defences and boosting its domestic vigilance in non-traditional security areas. The possibilities of religious deviation and trans-border terrorism merit attention. Brunei has shown that it can handle threats like the H1N1 pandemic, and other similar issues will be carefully addressed. It has, for example, an effective coordinating council for natural-disaster management. Threats to its natural resources are a recurring issue, especially as regards valuable stands of timber in isolated areas and marine resources threatened by illegal foreign fishermen. The regular prosecution of offenders is an indication that the mechanisms are in place to protect both the country's land and its marine interests.

Cambodia

Sokbunthoeun So

The year 2011 will be an important year for the ruling Cambodian People's Party (CPP), as it seeks to strengthen its position in preparation for the commune council elections due in 2012. These sub-national polls, introduced in 2002 as part of the country's "decentralization and deconcentration" (D&D) reforms, have importance comparable to that of the national legislative elections due to follow in 2013. Control of communes, the lowest level of local administration in Cambodia, is of high political significance to the CPP for two reasons.

First, control over local government provides an important structure for the operation of mass patronage. This control of local administration, together with well-organized networks and abundant financial and human resources, gives the CPP a powerful, patronage-oriented electoral machine. Under its former name — the People's Revolutionary Party of Kampuchea — the CPP maintained exclusive control over the country's communes throughout the 1980s. Despite the introduction of multi-party politics in a system of democratic governance, the party continued to exercise a great deal of control over them during much of the 1990s through the appointment of commune-level officials. It only opened up the commune posts to electoral competition by allowing the decentralization of local governance and polls for commune councils

CAMBODIA

Land Area:	181,040 sq. km.
Population (2009 World Bank data):	14,805,358
Capital:	Phnom Penh
Type of Government:	Parliamentary democracy and constitutional monarchy
Head of State:	King Norodom Sihamoni
Head of Government:	Prime Minister Hun Sen
Last Election:	2008
Next Election Due:	2013
Currency Used:	Riel
US$ Exchange Rate (2 December 2010):	US$1 = 4,050 riel

when it felt confident of electoral victory. When it finally allowed local-level electoral competition in the 2002 commune council elections, the CPP took 68.4 per cent of commune council seats nation-wide and 98.6 per cent — or 1,601 of the total 1,621 — of commune council chairmanships. In the 2007 commune council elections, it captured an even greater share of commune council seats, 70.4 per cent, along with 98.12 per cent or 1,591 commune council chairmanships.

Second, with further D&D reforms, which allowed indirect election to posts at higher levels of sub-national administration in Cambodia, commune councils become even more important. The 11,353 commune council members now form the bulk of the membership of the electoral colleges that elect district- and provincial-level office holders. This role comes in addition to the councils' power to appoint village chiefs and to elect members of the Cambodian Senate. With an overwhelming majority of commune councilors belonging to the CPP and the CPP's strong party discipline, the 2009 district and provincial council elections delivered a landslide victory to the party.

The CPP's work to strengthen its position in the coming commune council election will involve various strategies likely to weaken further Cambodia's already fragile opposition parties, whose lack of unity has already seen them in slow decline since 1998. This situation suggests that meaningful opposition politics in Cambodia may be over and that opposition parties may only exist at the behest of the ruling party. The CPP's strategy of co-optation and marginalization of potential competitors proved quite successful in the 2008 legislative election. It will be repeated in future elections, including sub-national elections.

The CPP strategy of co-optation seems to have had a significant impact in breaking the so-called "urban front" in which many opposition supporters had been concentrated. During the 2008 legislative elections, Prime Minister Hun Sen authorized all high-ranking CPP officials to appoint any defectors from the Sam Rainsy Party (SRP) as their advisors. One prominent case of such a political buy-off involved the SRP's chief of Commune Kilometer 6, Sok Sambath, who was appointed an advisor to the Prime Minister.

The strategy of marginalization through the use of legal procedures, as in the case of various lawsuits brought against various members of opposition parties, has done serious damage to the opposition parties and will likely continue. The SRP, which is the only major opposition party, suffered considerably from having its members, including Sam Rainsy himself, embroiled in successive lawsuits. Rainsy, who is now in exile, was convicted in two separate cases. He was charged with destruction of public property after his removal of a few Cambodia-Vietnam border markers in an October 2009 protest against alleged Vietnamese encroachment on Cambodian soil, and was sentenced to two years imprisonment by Svay Rieng Provincial court. He was again charged for disinformation and falsification of public documents after having published evidence of "alleged Vietnamese encroachment on Cambodian territory in video press conferences and on the SRP's website" and was sentenced by the Phnom Penh Municipal Court to ten years imprisonment and required to pay more than US$15,000 in fines and damages to the state. At the time of writing, he faced yet another court summons, on a separate lawsuit filed by Foreign Minister Hor Nam Hong two years ago.

For at least two reasons, the end of meaningful opposition politics does not suggest Cambodia's complete forsaking of electoral politics. First, ruling-party elites have accepted electoral competition as a source of both local and international legitimacy. Electoral competition is now a part of the game in Cambodia's governance. Second, these same elites are highly confident that the presence of the opposition is no longer a threat and they are able to win successive elections without many constraints, thanks to the perfection of their patronage-based electoral machine. The end of meaningful opposition, however, suggests that the final outcome of the democratic experiment begun in the early 1990s is a one-party electoral-autocratic state.

This weakening of the political opposition occurs in the context of an increasingly affluent ruling party, one that shows growing intolerance toward dissenting views. At the same time, the CPP seems to have done relatively well in bringing political stability and delivering services to the people, not least through a political patronage machine that co-opts potential rivals and expands the party's base of support at the grass-roots level.

Political stability, the main achievement of the Cambodian state-building process since the early 1990s, will continue to feature prominently in Cambodia under the CPP. It rests on a very strong ruling party, a very weak political opposition, and the ability of the ruling party's members to maintain internal cohesion. Very little internal CPP strife has become publicly known. Notwithstanding these conditions, the CPP's lack of a rule for leadership succession or clear guidelines for the selection of the party leader suggests a possible source of tension that could affect both the party's solidarity and the country's current political stability.

The mass-based patronage strategy of the CPP, although conceived to help the party sustain its legitimate power under an electoral regime, does have some trickle-down effect. Certain resources do benefit local people. And 79 per cent of Cambodians feel that the country is moving in the right direction, according to a 2009 International Republican Institute survey of Cambodian public opinion. Among the main reasons for this positive perception of the country's direction, survey respondents mentioned the construction of more roads, more schools, more medical facilities, and more temples (in descending order of importance). The private funds of CPP affiliates, including tycoons, have financed most of this construction. The party has claimed credit for these achievements with its campaign slogan, which calls it the only party that "gets things done".

Indonesia

Bernhard Platzdasch

Remaking Indonesia's public institutions and improving their quality remain possibly the most severe challenges facing the administration of President Susilo Bambang Yudhoyono. The country's swift transition to democratic rule and status as the world's largest Muslim-majority democracy long clouded over a reality that is now becoming increasingly clear: the New Order's institutional legacy and patrimonial style of politics have left a mark on the country that is difficult to shed. Democracy notwithstanding, the post–New Order state continues to endow well-heeled and politically linked business-people with favours. Indonesia's legal system has remained largely dysfunctional; the achievement of democracy has done little to strengthen the rule of law. Politics remains in the hands of oligarchic elites whose main interest remains access to state resources. Wide sections of the bureaucracy are in a state of disarray and performing poorly.

One main impediment to a more consolidated and targeted reform agenda is the President himself. Yudhoyono has consistently favoured a consensus-oriented style. He is unlikely to give up this preference during the remainder of his term. Despite his often maligned meekness, however, the President remains popular. One main reason for his popularity is his government's success in bringing about price stability, an essential criterion for an electorate for whom bread and butter issues count as a major concern. If the Yudhoyono administration can sustain its momentum in the run-up to the 2014 elections, the prospects for the President's Democrat Party remain good, even when that party

INDONESIA

Land Area:	1,919,440 sq. km.
Population (2009 World Bank data):	229,964,723
Capital:	Jakarta
Type of Government:	Presidential republic
Head of State:	President Susilo Bambang Yudhoyono
Last Election:	2009
Next Election:	2014
Currency Used:	Rupiah
US$ Exchange Rate (2 December 2010):	US$1 = 9,015 rupiah

fields a new presidential candidate. Incumbent party Chairman Anas Urbaningrum currently seems to be the figure being groomed to take over from Yudhoyono.

A second impediment to the consolidation of reform efforts is an underperforming Parliament, an institution with little hope of improvement in the near future. The last national elections took place only a year ago, in 2009, but political parties are already preoccupied with preparations for the 2014 polls. This year has seen a widening gulf between the President and his coalition partner Golkar, partly because Golkar chairman and magnate Aburizal Bakrie harbours ambitions to become the next president. Having received the endorsement of his candidacy from one regional Golkar chapter in 2010, Bakrie can expect more during 2011.

As Golkar became a more unreliable coalition partner for the President's party, the role of Islamic-oriented and Islamist parties such as the Justice and Prosperity Party (PKS) could become increasingly important in 2011. The PKS is now the largest Islamist party in Indonesia. It has recently pledged to become a fully open and pluralist party. The year ahead will make clearer whether it is indeed willing to shed the more problematic anti-Western and anti-Christian aspects of its doctrine. Among parties without an Islamic orientation, the PDIP or Indonesian Democratic Party of Struggle will eventually have to settle on whether the position of party chairman should stay within the Sukarno family — through the selection of the daughter of current chairman Megawati Sukarnoputri — or not.

A further impediment to Indonesia's ability to build on its democratic success lies in the area of governance at the sub-national level. Recent research has shown that decentralization has not been the cure-all for which many had hoped in the early democratic period. The future will bring exceedingly complex and multi-layered dynamics among decentralization, democratization, and globalization. Rivalries among national and local political players and aspirants will only complicate these dynamics. Indonesia is a stable and open democracy, but corruption and "money politics" remain rampant. Political aspirants who have "paid" their way into office often have little interest in delivering on their campaign promises. As a result, instead of bringing about closer ties between officials and citizens, decentralization has meant that Indonesians' level of trust in their representatives continues to shrink.

Democracy and decentralization have not destroyed the relations of power that characterized the New Order. They have, rather, often allowed them to flourish. Paradoxically, however, local elites would be among those with the most to lose from a return to the centralized authoritarianism of the New Order years. They will therefore remain keen supporters of democracy. Jostling over local power and control looks likely to remain a critical and potentially volatile issue for Indonesia for many years to come. The next several years will also make clear whether Indonesia will suffer the type of local bossism that has crippled countries such as Thailand and the Philippines.

Another challenge for Indonesia during 2011 and beyond is to bring its military under complete civil control. The military no longer claims a right to a formal political role. It is no longer represented in Parliament. But it has retained its territorial command structure, and its involvement in business activities is still far too extensive for it to be respected as a professional force. Another persistent legacy from the

New Order is that civilian politicians at all levels still recruit retired officers to run for their parties. This severe malaise is unlikely to be overcome any time in the near future.

Perhaps more severe than malaise, among the issues that the Yudhoyono government must address in 2011, is rising religious intolerance and the challenge of living up to its assertion that it guarantees freedom of religion. Religious minorities and sects such as the Ahmadiyah increasingly face Islamist bullying and persecution. But Yudhoyono has been wary about taking a clear stance on matters that could damage his popularity among supporters. The President has tried to embrace the conservative Muslim vote since he took office in 2004. He curbed the activities of the Ahmadiyah and helped to push the Islamist-backed anti-pornography law. Parliament is set to readdress the Ahmadiyah issue in the coming months. The likely outcome of its deliberations is a formal ban on Ahmadiyah. Another disquieting sign is that Islamist vigilante groups increasingly rub shoulders with local politicians and the police. Religious freedom in Indonesia requires that politicians stop using Islamist fringe groups for their own ends. It also requires that the government extend official recognition beyond the six currently recognized religions to other beliefs and abolish a 1965 law on the "Prevention of Misuse or Desecration of Religion". An exertion of more resolute leadership on the part of President Yudhoyono would very much help Indonesia ensure religious freedom.

The successful prosecution of Abu Bakar Bashir, the former emir of Southeast Asia's largest jihadist Islamist group, Jemaah Islamiyah, has been vital to Indonesia's efforts to eradicate terrorism. It is now up to the prosecutors at Bashir's trial next year to provide convincing evidence that he did indeed instigate terrorist acts, particularly as many mainstream Muslim leaders are often inclined to avoid criticizing a fellow Muslim.

Indonesia remains distinctly more inward-looking than other large Asian countries. Tellingly, for example, the number of Indonesian immigrants and students in the United States remains far lower than the figure for India or China. In the years ahead, however, Indonesia looks set gently to counterbalance Asia's leading nations, China, India, and Japan. U.S. President Barack Obama's visit to Indonesia in late 2010 proved a good opportunity for placing Indonesia on the map and helping the country to gain greater clout in global affairs. Perhaps even more important, an improvement of U.S.–Indonesian relations can be instrumental to building the bridge of trust that was severely lacking during the administration of George W. Bush.

Laos

Ian Baird

It is always extremely difficult to know what is happening politically in the Lao People's Democratic Republic. The media are tightly controlled by the state, although in recent years some reporters have become a bit more daring than was previously the norm. This relative daring is especially evident in critiques of particular development policies and projects. Still, when reporting about the government and the Lao People's Democratic Party, the media release only official government-sanctioned news. Rumours originating from various sources frequently circulate in Vientiane and elsewhere in the country, but it is almost always difficult to confirm their veracity. While the country has adopted significant economic reforms since the adoption of its "New Economic Mechanism" in 1986, there has been little structural political reform. At least for the foreseeable future, there are no signs that significant political change will come to Laos. The country is likely to remain a one-party state, and to continue to be one of the ASEAN member states that are most difficult to understand.

Powerful patronage networks remain an important part of the political landscape in Laos, and corruption is becoming increasingly common. There is now a larger pie to divide up, after all. And the "revolutionary fire", which was more evident in the early years after the present government took control of the country in 1975, has dimmed considerably in recent years. Corruption is bound to be

LAOS

Land Area:	236,800 sq. km.
Population (2009 World Bank data):	6,320,429
Capital:	Vientiane
Type of Government:	Communist people's democratic republic
Head of State and General Secretary of the Lao People's Revolutionary Party:	President Choummaly Sayasone
Head of Government:	Prime Minister Bouasone Bouphavanh
Last Election:	2006
Next Election:	2011
Currency Used:	Kip
US$ Exchange Rate (2 December 2010):	US$1 = 8,010 kip

common in a system that, like that in Laos today, lacks transparency and accountability but at the same time promotes liberal economic policies, policies founded on the promotion of foreign investment and of export-oriented business activities.

The planned Don Sahong Hydropower Project in the Khone Falls area of Champasak Province, in the country's deep south, exemplifies Laos' accountability problems. The project is being proposed for development by a Malaysian company, Mega-First Corporation Berhad. It also enjoys the strong support of the family of the former President of Laos, Khamtay Siphandone. His son Sonxay Siphandone currently serves as Governor of Champasak. Sonxay was apparently slated to become Minister of the Prime Minister's Office. He has so far not been transferred to that post, however, possibly because he may be in a better position to protect his family's interests in the Don Sahong Dam by remaining in power in Champasak.

Despite considerable concern within Laos regarding the potentially negative impact of the project on important fish migrations in the Mekong River, the Siphandone family has been able to curtail open debate on this impact. Sonxay has told senior provincial government officials in Champasak that criticism of the project would not be tolerated. At a 2010 meeting of those officials, he stated that, for the country to develop, all Laotian people would need to remain in solidarity with regard to important development projects like the Don Sahong Dam. The Siphandone family's support for the Don Sahong Dam project appears to be linked to more than the desire to develop the nation, however. According to Laotian sources close to the project, the behind-the-scenes project manager is Khamtay Siphandone's son-in-law, although he has a "front man" working for him as the official manager. The Siphandone family is expected to gain significant benefits if the project moves ahead.

Similarly, the Vientiane government has successfully stifled criticism of its flagship hydropower project, the Nam Theun 2 Dam (NT2) in central Laos, which enjoys the support of the World Bank and the Asian Development Bank (ADB). Recent reports note serious downstream impact along the Xe Bang Fai River, caused by poor quality water released from the dam's large reservoir. This impact includes human and animal health problems, as well as steep declines in downstream fisheries. Nevertheless, both those responsible for the project and the Laotian media have remained largely silent. Many foreign observers, including some prominent academics, have also failed to grasp the serious risks associated with NT2. The World Bank has often defended the project when substantive criticisms have been raised, thus both compromising its credibility and preventing critical dialogue regarding the dam. Still, even the skilled public relations officers of the World Bank and the project are unlikely to be able to keep the truth hidden. Officials from the ADB and the nearby Theun-Hinboun Hydropower Project could not, after all, prevent word of the serious social and environmental impact associated with that dam from emerging more than a decade ago.

Another of the serious challenges facing Laos today and in the immediate future relates to the granting of large-scale land concessions. In recent years, a flood of land-concession agreements have been granted, mainly to foreign investors. These latter have included many from neighbouring countries like Vietnam, China, and Thailand. The concessions provide for the cultivation of various annual and perennial export crops; they include tree plantations. Hundreds of thousands of hectares of rubber plantations have been developed. Much of this development has resulted in the displacement of rural people who previously farmed the land granted to investors or used former forest lands that have been now converted to commercial use. Many upland minorities have found themselves without crucial sources of livelihood, and, to add insult to injury, the displaced people who work for the land concession-holders often find themselves suffering exploitative labour conditions.

Many villagers have protested against the changes caused by land concessions. In May 2007, in response to concerns raised regarding these concessions, Prime Minister Bouasone Bouphavanh ordered a temporary halt to new concessions. The central government decreed that district and provincial governments could no longer grant large land concessions on their own. The main critic of large land concessions within the government appears to be Khamouane Boupha, the minister responsible for the relatively new National Land Management Authority (NLMA). Despite his important role in orchestrating the communist take-over of the country in 1975, the former left-leaning neutralist military leader is allegedly the only minister in the government who is not a member of the Party.

The land situation in Laos illustrates a number of broader realities of the country's political circumstances. First, the initial moratorium on issuing new land concessions in Laos was never very effective, thus illustrating the lack of power of the Prime Minister. Second, there are significant divisions among senior political figures regarding land issues. Some members of the National Assembly have also been vocal in their condemnation of concessions. Their actions have demonstrated that the National Assembly is beginning to function in a watch-dog capacity, whereas in the past it was largely seen as a rubber stamp for government initiatives. Nevertheless, other senior politicians clearly remain supportive of large land concessions. Some have indeed positioned themselves and their families to take advantage of the ongoing land grabbing.

It is hard to know how the situation will ultimately play itself out, but from mid-2009 concessions were again officially granted, following the release of revised guidelines. Although these guidelines specified that concessions over 150 hectares required NLMA approval, within just a few weeks opposition from parts of the government, including members of the National Assembly, forced a renewed moratorium on land concessions. Weaker than the first moratorium, this second moratorium only affects concessions larger than 1,000 hectares. Furthermore, exceptions to the rules are granted frequently. As the *Vientiane Times* reported, "if an urgent case arises, with an investor needing more than 1,000 hectares of land to carry out a business, the sectors concerned will advise the cabinet in making a decision".

Malaysia

Barry Wain

If economically Malaysia is caught in a middle-income trap, as the government says, politically the country is in deeper trouble. Half a century of nation building is eking away almost imperceptibly behind a seemingly endless stream of vicious political rhetoric.

Malaysia is not going to collapse anytime soon. While weakened, its foundations are still relatively strong, and the economy is lubricated by the exploitation of oil and gas deposits, though those, too, are dwindling. The majority of Malaysians, including a solid middle class, remain moderate and unwilling to allow the country to be torn apart. But, unless the decline is halted, the symptoms of trouble will continue to be felt, in ways big and small: an ongoing exodus of talented people and capital, a sense of alienation among remaining Malaysians not on the gravy train, and a wariness on the part of foreign investors who crave certainty.

MALAYSIA

Land Area:	330,434 sq. km.
Population (2009 World Bank data):	27,467,837
Capital:	Kuala Lumpur (Administrative capital: Putrajaya)
Type of Government:	Federated parliamentary democracy and constitutional monarchy
Head of State:	Yang Di-Pertuan Agong Tuanku Mizan Zainal Abidin
Head of Government:	Prime Minister Dato' Seri Mohd Najib bin Tun Haji Abdul Razak
Last Election:	2008
Next Election Due:	2013
Currency Used:	Ringgit (RM)
US$ Exchange Rate (2 December 2010):	US$1 = RM4.15

While lacking the street clashes and violence of neighbouring Thailand, Malaysia similarly faces an uncertain future because of the increasing inability of its people to coexist and cooperate. The fabric of Malaysian society is fraying as fissures widen between the main ethnic communities — the majority Malays, asserting their status as indigenous, and the Chinese and Indians, historically regarded as immigrant — over the notion and practice that with indigenousness come privileges.

The old social contract, imagined or real, which dates from independence in 1957, works less and less satisfactorily, and there is little agreement on the way forward. After forty years of affirmative action to help Malays compete, many Chinese and Indians have had enough. But, on their part, numbers of Malays insist on retaining their privileges as "special rights".

What may eventually become the death of multiracialism is a slow and insidious process that infects the Malaysian soul. It manifests itself in coarsening public exchanges, often racially inflammatory; growing distrust among the communities; and silence about the whispered hope, in past decades, of creating one *bangsa Malaysia*, a Malaysian nation.

The spreading malaise has undermined the fourteen-party National Front government, dominated by the United Malays National Organisation (UMNO) and including its original core partners, the Malaysian Chinese Association (MCA) and the Malaysian Indian Congress MIC). Chinese Malaysians have deserted the MCA in protest, essentially, against UMNO domination. The MIC is likewise a fairly empty shell.

While UMNO clings to power, frequently by playing on Malay insecurities, the party shows few signs of taking the decisive action required to treat the decay in public life. Indeed, UMNO itself is in dire need of reform, along with sections of the bureaucracy and state institutions that have become complacent and compromised after more than fifty years of UMNO-dominated, coalition rule.

Prime Minister Najib Razak's long record as an UMNO loyalist means that it was probably unrealistic to expect him to deliver reformist leadership when he took over in April 2009. And there is no reason to believe that he will do so any time soon. In keeping with his instincts, refined across thirty-five years in politics, he has proceeded cautiously and pragmatically, limiting bold forays to the realm of foreign policy — for example, by improving relations with Singapore and cozying up to Washington.

For a premier who arrived loudly proclaiming the slogan "One Malaysia", suggesting a commitment to arrest the deterioration in race relations, Najib has disappointed many observers. While he has tried to articulate a vision of a more inclusive society, he has failed to stop influential elements in UMNO from engaging in blatant race-baiting. So obvious is the gap between the vision articulated and the race-baiting practiced that political analysts offer two possible explanations: that the Prime Minister is being challenged by factions within UMNO, or that he is engaged in a calculated campaign to win non-Malay votes while his colleagues attract Malay support. The truth may be a little bit of both.

No doubt Najib has encountered strong Malay resistance to his declared desire to modify Malaysia's affirmative action programmes in order to uplift all needy groups. But while he has hesitated, Malay entitlement groups opposed to any relaxation of the pro-Malay policy have proliferated. The presence and number of these groups are likely to make his task so much harder.

Although Najib talks incessantly of the need to change, he has mostly settled for the status quo. It has become characteristic of him to advertise a proposed initiative, only to back down as the deadline to commit to it approaches. While he has finally bitten the bullet on reducing or eliminating pervasive subsidies, they will be phased out only over an extended period. And if he ever goes ahead with a goods and services tax, considered necessary to widen the country's tax base, it is likely to be greeted with a measure of disbelief, so often has its introduction been postponed.

Unlike his predecessor Abdullah Badawi, Najib does not lack energy. With the help of a slew of highly-paid foreign consultants, he has pinpointed many of the problems plaguing the country. But his efforts to address them often appear to be superficial or gimmicky, as solutions proposed rarely tackle underlying causes.

Typically, the government has established a Talent Corporation to entice home some of the 700,000 Malaysians who, according to official figures, live abroad. But in the absence of improvements on the ground — in quality of life, including a safe and clean environment, in sound public infrastructure and services, and in education and an end to ethnic discrimination — the programme is unlikely to be any more successful than two similar initiatives in the past fifteen years. Those initiatives attracted fewer than 1,000 returnees.

Despite ritual denunciations of the old way of doing business, available evidence indicates Najib has not been able to dismantle or bypass the entrenched patronage networks that envelop UMNO. For instance, his administration awarded a well-connected company a large plot of land in Kuala Lumpur in what turned out to be a private — as well as a privatization — deal. The official justification for breeching the promise to call for open tenders: the company was the first to propose the development, which happens to be the same reason used at the height of cronyism in the 1980s and 1990s. And, when the opposition accused the government of awarding the contract to build the Malaysian King's new RM935 million palace to an UMNO-linked company, the government had another excuse for the lack of open tendering: security concerns.

In different circumstances, the next general election, which must be held by 2013, might end the uncertainty. But this is doubtful at Malaysia's current point of political evolution.

The multiracial opposition Pakatan Rakyat coalition, led by former deputy premier Anwar Ibrahim, has found the going tough since it made striking gains and deprived the National Front of its customary two-thirds majority in Parliament in the 2008 election. Pakatan Rakyat's image has been tarnished by bickering within and between component parties and its less than stellar performance in administering the four states that it controls. To be fair, the opposition has also been targeted by a federal government prepared to play dirty to retain office, and by central government control of almost everything except land and water. The state administrations are thus rendered fairly helpless and chronically short of funds.

Realistically, not much will change in Malaysia if UMNO and its allies extend their unbroken rule. If Pakatan Rakyat overcomes overwhelming odds and breaks the National Front stranglehold, that will settle some questions but open many others.

Myanmar

Tin Maung Maung Than

Myanmar's political outlook appeared grim during the two decades following its election of May 1990. The National League for Democracy

MYANMAR

Land Area:	678,675 sq. km.
Population (2008 World Bank data):	49,600,000 (estimates for 2010 as high as 55,000,000)
Capital:	Naypyitaw
Type of Government:	Military government, in transition to constitutional regime
Head of State:	Senior General Than Shwe
Head of Government:	Prime Minister Thein Sein
Last Election:	2010
Next Election:	2015
Currency Used:	Kyat
US$ Exchange Rate (2 December 2010):	US$1 = 6.14 kyat (official rate)

(NLD) won more than 80 per cent of the unicameral parliamentary seats in that election, only to be denied the right to form a government by the ruling junta. During the ensuing twenty years of confrontation between the NLD-led opposition and the military rulers, the hallmark of the country's politics was "more of the same", along with occasional unrealized hopes of "breakthrough". The seven-step Road Map announced in August 2003 by the then Prime Minister on behalf of the State Peace and Development Council (SPDC) elicited some hope and excitement among those expecting change. But, as the concomitant constitution-making process unfolded with strong indications of continuing military control, the NLD and all those rooting for liberal democracy quickly became disillusioned with the stage-managed political transition envisaged by the SPDC. Hence, Myanmar's new constitution passed overwhelmingly by a national referendum in May 2008 — in the aftermath of the devastating Cyclone Nargis, which caused more than 130,000 deaths — was found to be unacceptable to the NLD and pro-democracy stakeholders as well as the Western states.

The elections held on 7 November 2010, in accordance with the 2008 Constitution, yet again stirred up the moribund political ambience of Myanmar. Calls came for an "inclusive" process leading to a "free and fair" election from domestic stakeholders (including the NLD, newly formed parties, and ethnic nationalities) and democracy lobbies both in the West and in the region. ASEAN, the United Nations, and Western states led by the United States took the lead in making such calls. Among the many demands put to the SPDC in the run-up to the elections were to repeal or amend electoral laws seen as favouring the newly-formed Union Solidarity and Development Party (USDP). That party had been formed from the Union Solidarity and Development Association, a mass-based social organization created by the junta. These laws were seen to penalize other parties. The junta was also called on to release some 2,000 "political prisoners" and NLD leader Aung San Suu Kyi and allow them to participate in the elections; to allow international observers to monitor the elections; and to allow free access to the elections on the part of foreign media personnel. Eventually, the NLD refused to re-register for the elections. It was thus dissolved in accordance with the provisions of the election laws.

Nevertheless, the SPDC stayed its course and withstood all criticism and even condemnation from detractors. The boycott campaign against the elections staged by the now-defunct NLD and its allies, as well as expatriate dissidents, failed to derail the electoral process. Thirty-seven political parties, including a breakaway faction of the NLD, fielded 3,071 candidates to contest 1,157 seats (polls in another six constituencies were cancelled because of security problems). These seats included those in the two national parliaments, the Pyithu Hluttaw or lower house and Amyotha Hluttaw or upper house, and fourteen regional parliaments, seven for Bamar-majority regions and seven for ethnic states. Among them, fifty-five constituencies were walk-overs by single candidates facing no challengers. As expected, the USDP won the majority in both national legislatures. It garnered close to 80 per cent of the contested constituencies, a result that translated into nearly 60 per cent of total seats; 25 per cent of seats are reserved for military nominees.

In the Bamar-majority regions, previously called divisions, the USDP's majority in the provincial legislatures was even larger, with shares hovering around 90 per cent of contested seats in six regions and around 80 per cent in Yangon Region. In the Kayah State it scored a perfect record. In the other six ethnic majority states, ethnic-based parties carved out a substantial share of the constituencies, but the USDP still managed to win 40 to 60 per cent of constituencies at the polls. When combined with the military share of 25 per cent, the USDP could attain a decisive majority in those states' legislatures as well.

What does this election portend for the political future of Myanmar? One should not expect accelerated political or economic reforms in the short term. Myanmar will have a constitutional government under an executive presidency. There will be some opposition voices in the bicameral national parliament, while the executive branch will be dominated by retired and serving senior military officers and technocrats chosen by the military. This is not a power-sharing exercise but a power distribution exercise within the ruling elite: there will be pluralism and a flatter power structure, but the military's institutional and personal grip on power will be maintained. As the following points suggest, the SPDC has ensured that everything is stacked in favour of continuing military control and influence over the vital functions of the Myanmar state. It will continue its tradition of extending its authority beyond what is required by national defence and bordering on being a political entity, as the guarantor as well as the embodiment of state authority.

The Tatmadaw (Myanmar Defence Services, or MDS) has the following prerogatives, as accorded by the provisions of the 2008 Constitution:

- Complete military autonomy to manage its own affairs.
- Designation of the military Commander-in-Chief (C-in-C) as supreme commander of all armed forces.
- Requirement for the President to be "well acquainted with the affairs of the Union such as political, administrative, economic and military".

- Reserved seats for the military in the form of C-in-C's nominees amounting to 25 per cent of the seats in both houses of the national parliament.
- Reserved seats for the military in the form of C-in-C's nominees amounting to one-third of the elected representatives in the parliaments of the (fourteen) states and regions comprising the Union.
- Military representatives slated for six out of eleven members of the National Defence and Security Council.
- Reserved positions for the nominees of the C-in-C as ministers and deputy ministers for defence, home affairs and border areas.
- Exemption for military personal to remain in military service while serving as ministers and deputy ministers, whereas civilians have to resign from their positions as parliamentarians or civil servants and suspend their party affiliations.
- The President, after coordinating with the National Defence and Security Council, may declare a national emergency and then hand over executive, legislative, and judicial powers to the C-in-C "if there is sufficient reason for a state of emergency to arise that may disintegrate the Union or that may cause the loss of sovereignty, due to acts or attempts to take over the sovereignty of the Union by insurgency, violence and wrongful forcible means".
- "All the armed forces in the Union shall be under the command of the Defence Services".

Nevertheless, there are indications that a new dynamic is likely to emerge within the military under the new power configuration. The much-anticipated change to third-generation leaders would bring in a fresh cohort of generals who are some two decades younger than the cohort that commanded the MDS in the era of the 1990 elections. Furthermore, the powerful regional commanders would no longer be entitled to exercise executive power in their respective territories; they would only be vested with authority over military matters. The chief ministers, who are presidential appointees, would hold sway over the administration of the fourteen states and regions, whose territorial boundaries overlap with corresponding regional military commands. A new modus vivendi must thus be worked out both between regional commanders and chief ministers, many of the latter of whom may turn out to be retired generals senior to the former, and between regional commanders and line ministries under ministers, who are also likely to be retired senior generals. Both the chief ministers and cabinet ministers are to be appointed by the Executive President. Moreover, regional and state parliaments are also expected to play a role in the political governance of their respective areas, especially in the six states where ethnic parties and their allies would hold some 30 to 50 per cent of the total parliamentary seats. Hence, this new structure of provincial authority is completely different from the familiar top-down command structure exercised by the regional commanders in the SPDC era.

All in all, the introduction of a form of pluralism in the body politic and a relatively flatter power distribution poses new challenges and presents fresh opportunities to the MDS in post-election Myanmar. One step removed from direct political governance, the new Tatmadaw leadership could devote more attention, time, and energy to enhancing professionalism in the MDS. This outcome may well be the initial step toward developing a new paradigm for civil-military relations in Myanmar, one conducive to nation-building and human security.

How the legislative process and governance at the centre (in Naypyitaw) and in the provinces (in the regional/state capitals) unfold will depend upon the military's degree of comfort with the new structures and processes. It will also depend on the behaviour of the "opposition" in and outside of parliament. The military remains the crucial agent of change or its lack. The best hope for the country is the "socialization" of the military into a new "political culture" of debate and discussion, a far cry from the top-down apex structure to which it has been accustomed for decades. It will be an uphill task for the democrats and their allies at home and abroad.

The determination of NLD leader Aung San Suu Kyi, who was released from house arrest on 13 November, to continue her quest for human rights, democracy, and the rule of law, along with the refusal of the NLD to stop its activities after being dissolved, are going to pose difficult problems for the new government. Her support for the convening of the so-called Second Panlong Conference to forge unity among the pro-democracy forces and ethnic nationalities is likely to be seen as a contravention of the 2008 Constitution and a challenge to the new government's authority. It may result in further confrontation despite her conciliatory overtures for dialogue and cooperation with the junta and all other stakeholders in Myanmar's political arena.

As recent outbreaks of fighting between a breakaway faction of the Democratic Kayin Buddhist Army, a Kayin ceasefire group (most of whose members had agreed to be subsumed under MDS command), show, the problem of the transformation of the military arms of the recalcitrant ceasefire groups (Kachin, Wa, and some Shan and Kayin factions) will have to be tackled intelligently and magnanimously by the new government. Otherwise, the transformation could degenerate into civil war.

Despite Aung San Suu Kyi's expressed willingness to review the impact of sanctions on the Myanmar people and to consider the possibility of the lifting of sanctions in order to improve the lot of the polity, the issue could turn out to be contentious. The process could be bogged down by acrimonious debates and hard lobbying, even if an in-principle consensus could be achieved. United States–led sanctions on the part of the European Union and other Western states are also likely to remain in place in the short term, as these governments' condemnation of the outcome of the recent elections leave them unwilling to "normalize" relations with Myanmar.

The Philippines

Maria Ortuoste

Another Aquino, another possibility. The election to the Philippine presidency of Benigno "Noynoy" Aquino III in May 2010, along with the relatively quick vote-count that followed the polls, has led a majority of Filipinos to be more optimistic about their personal lives and the national situation. But Filipinos have been here before.

THE PHILIPPINES

Land Area:	298,170 sq. km.
Population (2009 World Bank data):	91,983,102
Capital:	Manila
Type of Government:	Presidential republic
Head of State:	President Benigno S. Aquino III
Last Election:	2010
Next Election:	2013 (congressional elections)
Currency Used:	Philippine peso
US$ Exchange Rate (2 December 2010):	US$1 = PhP43.75

Presidents from Ferdinand Marcos to Gloria Macapagal Arroyo have promised a "new society", only to fail because of personal venality, institutional inefficiencies, military defiance, or political shenanigans. Aquino — popularly known as PNoy (pronounced "pee-noy") — needs to surmount these legacies of disappointment, to live up to his father's ideals and to learn from his mother's experience.

Aquino has promised to deliver good governance as the foundation for a peaceful and stable environment, one conducive to economic growth and, eventually, social transformation. Will he succeed? Will he stay the course? These are the important questions for Filipinos. One author cannot make claims of prescience, but it would be fair to say that in the short term, we will see a measure of *necessary instability*. "Instability", because instilling good-governance practices means undertaking measures bound to "destabilize" business and politics as usual. "Necessary", because Aquino's credibility and the country's future are at stake. Aquino faces four major challenges — addressing the situation in Mindanao, demonstrating leadership, forging partnerships, and revitalizing institutions.

Like other Philippine presidents, Aquino needs to address Mindanao's future. On the plus side, the government is seriously thinking of an overarching framework to address the needs of all Mindanaons. Aquino has also identified good governance, the effective delivery of basic services, sustainable development, and security-sector reform as the pillars of the Mindanao peace framework. In pursuing the peace process, the government can tap the International Contact Group in the case of any impasse, the NGO-led Civilian Protection Component to deliver assistance, and possibly the International Monitoring Team to provide a measure of security and transparency.

On the negative side, the government still needs to develop a well-coordinated political, developmental, legislative, and public relations strategy on Mindanao. Otherwise, broken promises, such as amending the constitution to accommodate claims to ancestral domains, will be used as proof of government insincerity and pretexts to stall negotiations.

On this issue and others, decisive and focused leadership will be fundamental. Even as Aquino demonstrates his mettle, his "virtue" and capability will be questioned. The compliance of Hacienda Luisita — the vast Central Luzon plantation of the Cojuangco family, to which his mother Corazon Aquino belonged — with the agrarian reform law needs to be settled. Aquino cannot forsake responsibility by saying that he only has a one per cent share in the "corporation" that owns the estate. Charges of corruption and illegal gambling will continue to be raised against his close associates, but unless charges are made against the President himself, he should be able to weather these allegations. The more important question is whether they will distract the government from its domestic agenda.

Aquino's competence will also be questioned. Already criticized for his "tepid" performance as a member of the Philippine Senate, Aquino has faced additional criticism for his government's handling of the August 2010 hostage-taking episode in Manila in which a number of tourists from Hong Kong were killed. Presenting the investigative committee's findings to the Chinese Government prior to its public release in the Philippines may have mollified China and Hong Kong, but it raised questions about his own transparency — one of the virtues on which his presidential campaign was based.

Nonetheless, Aquino may prove to be a quick study. Despite lapses, the investigative committee completed its task on time. Major projects such as the anti-corruption effort, prosecuting "tax evaders", creating a justice commission to investigate the Arroyo administration's excesses, and putting the Mindanao negotiating panel together were undertaken within his first hundred days in office. More importantly, Aquino reassigned top military officials close to the Arroyo administration and called on the military to respect the country's democratic institutions over and above personality. The emphasis on institutions is, if anything, refreshing and heartening.

Institutional inefficiencies and organizational malaise present Aquino with a third set of challenges. The President has removed or is reviewing Arroyo's "midnight appointments", and he has appointed talented people to Cabinet posts. The internal revenue and customs bureaux have been especially energetic in pursuing tax evaders and smugglers. Going after the "big fish" makes for good newspaper copy, but the real question is how long these impressive and energetic efforts will last. Top officials serve at the pleasure of the President. Actual implementation relies on mid-level bureaucrats, poorly-paid employees, and possibly disgruntled police and military officials. While many public servants are honest and hard-working, there are unscrupulous officials who can wait out the inevitable changing of the guard. The administration has said that it will not tolerate poor performance and corruption in the ranks. Accordingly, it has established a Citizens' Concerns Website and promoted "digital volunteerism". But greater transparency can only be effective if the government also implements a mechanism to weed out frivolous claims to protect the innocent, provides the resources for effective responses to serious reports of malfeasance, and ensures that reforms are sustained. It is still unclear whether organizations and bureaucracies can be so revitalized to increase public trust.

Without legal, social, and institutional foundations, transparency and good governance will only be mottoes *du jour*. To secure these foundations, Aquino needs to surmount the challenge of balancing disparate groups of supporters in the legislature, in local government, and in civil society. But into which partnerships to enter? And with whom? Right now, Philippine politics is in an odd zone: Old guards such as career and traditional politicians, and scions of political dynasties, share political space with a younger generation of legislators and local government leaders. Although they are still few, the most talented among the latter can become the catalysts and carriers of reform beyond the President's six-year term. But how can any one group among the President's backers commit to any other without putting its political credibility at risk?

In the legislature, Aquino's team reached a deal with Senate Speaker Juan Ponce Enrile whereby the President's Liberal Party, which lacks an effective majority in the Philippine Congress, obtained chairmanship of important senate committees — Finance, Ways and Means, Blue Ribbon, and Justice. At the same time, the administration's allies will have to deal with opposition from legislators in the Arroyo and Marcos coalitions. Time will tell whether Aquino will be able to attract and embolden a reformist spirit among the new legislators.

Reform at the local level will help sustain public approval. But will Aquino be able to attract entrenched local leaders without resorting to outright pay-offs or simply ignoring their excesses? It is highly probable that Aquino's team could reach out to local leaders — such as those in the provinces of Isabela, Ifugao, and Pampanga — known for practicing good governance. If the government is able to link top-down initiatives with bottom-up efforts, then it might just be possible for Aquino to plant the roots of reform at the local level.

These are just some of the issues that the Aquino government faces. It must also address the matter of law and order, the pending review of the Republic of the Philippines–United States Visiting Forces Agreement, and the question of how to deal with a more assertive and capable China. It is too early to say if the Philippines' current President Aquino will be successful. While much depends on his leadership and ability to coordinate strategies, there are factors beyond his control — the internal dynamics of the Moro Islamic Liberation Front and the Communist National Democratic Front, the people's patience to wait for long-term gains rather than enjoy short-term results, and even just plain luck.

In the near term, if Aquino and his team are able to "destabilize" traditional practices and introduce more progressive ways of thinking and to lay the foundations for revitalized institutions and a more effective bureaucracy, then we may say that he is actually doing his job. And maybe, just maybe, this short-term necessary instability will bring the Philippines what Aquino and the rest of Filipinos actually want: long-term stability based on good governance, openness, and a fully functional democracy.

Singapore

N. Ganesan

Singapore is generally regarded as the most developed and successful state in Southeast Asia. A good measure of the reason for this success has lain in a benign immediate external environment and in the ruling government's near total capture of domestic structures and political discourse. Yet its often admired developmental approach and the incumbent regime's control of the domestic political situation are likely to be challenged in a variety of ways in the future. Political scientists have long hypothesized that dominant party systems are structurally calibrated to fail. This outcome is owing to the fact that, even if they succeed for any length of time, their tendency to complacency leads to their eventual collapse. The examples of Japan, South Korea, and Taiwan appear to bear out this observation. Equally spectacular and closer to Singapore was the Barisan Nasional government's loss of five states to the opposition in the Malaysian elections of 2008. In Singapore's case, a combination of internally generated changes and externally driven ones is likely to challenge the incumbent government in the near future. Even in the famously well-ordered city state, structural changes may have regime consequences.

Of the internally generated changes none presents a greater challenge than the rising cost of living and the pattern of class stratification that is increasingly taking root. This situation is at least partly exacerbated

SINGAPORE

Land Area:	692 sq. km.
Population (2009 World Bank data):	4,987,600
Capital:	Singapore
Type of Government:	Parliamentary democracy
Head of State:	President S.R. Nathan
Head of Government:	Prime Minister Lee Hsien Loong
Last Election:	2006
Next Election Due:	2012
Currency Used:	Singapore dollar
US$ Exchange Rate (2 December 2010):	US$1 = S$1.31

by government policies pertaining to employment practices and immigration. Among externally generated changes, technological changes and the impact of globalization have given Singaporeans greater experience of political, economic, and social settings that differ from their country and greater opportunity to create a domain for political discourse beyond the reach of the regime.

Recent internal changes have been substantial. Singapore has experienced a significant rise in its cost of living compared to a generation ago. This rise is most apparent in precisely the three areas that propelled the People's Action Party (PAP) into unchallenged political power from the late 1960s — housing, health services, and education. Affordable public housing was one of the greatest achievements of the PAP government. It was skillfully designed and delivered with the retention of social cohesion very much in mind. This goal brought a policy of ethnic quotas and the provision of secondary facilities like markets, schools, community centres, and playgrounds in the immediate vicinity of Housing and Development Board (HDB) flats. HDB estates, housing approximately 85 per cent of the country's population, continue to be a global benchmark. However, during the course of the last two decades the prices of HDB flats, both for first-time buyers and for buyers in the secondary or resale market, have become expensive and in some cases unaffordable. The reason for this hike in property prices was lax controls on purchases, introduced to stimulate demand when there was a glut of new units on the market. These liberalized rules allowed for speculative purchases of HDB flats. The situation was exacerbated by liberal immigration rules, framed with the goal of increasing the population base of the country. As a result of these twin forces, housing prices rose at a rate disproportionate to wage adjustments. Since housing is one of the most basic demands of the resident population, the rise in housing prices has led to much frustration on the part of Singaporeans wishing to get married and start families. Whereas the government has recognized the situation and attempted to develop remedies, base prices have remained high relative to wages.

Health care costs have also risen substantially in Singapore. Part of the reason for this rise is the government's policy of restructuring public hospitals, to bring them into close alignment with private hospitals. It also began to implement a policy that sought to peg payment rates to the economic situation of individuals. The first practice led to a significant rise in medical costs, including the cost of basic primary care. Its consequences were made more severe as employers began to reduce the health benefits of their employees and as the nearly free medical and dental treatment previously afforded to school-going children was withdrawn. As a result of the confluence of these forces, health care in Singapore has become expensive. A common joke in local circles is that similar services and facilities can be had in Malaysia at half the cost and in Thailand for a quarter of the cost. Even the government appears to have recognized the situation. It is exploring ways to promote the better utilization of the funds in citizens' compulsory Medisave accounts. Seeking lower-cost medical treatment in neighbouring countries numbers among the solutions under consideration. Simple solutions might include subsidizing primary health care and introducing a nationwide health insurance scheme for school-going children. Singapore must be one of the few developed countries in the world not to have introduced the latter scheme, and the last thing that parents need is the trauma of a large medical bill on top of the anxiety of a major illness involving their children.

The third area in which the cost of living in Singapore has become higher relative to wages is education. There have been major changes in the educational system, centring on the introduction of a range of different types of schools. Quite apart from the Special Assistance Plan schools designed to train elites fluent in two languages, there are now a plethora of independent and semi-independent schools. These schools charge different basic rates, and, coupled with additional costs for tuition, transport, computers, and overseas tours, the monthly average cost of supporting a school-going child has become quite high. During the early years of PAP rule education in Singapore was extremely affordable. Education was regularly and quite justifiably regarded as the best way to achieve social mobility. Many of the PAP's first and second generation of leaders and high-ranking civil servants came from humble backgrounds and benefitted from these policies. Their backgrounds and history of mobility also left these leaders cognizant of issues at the ground level.

Social stratification has become an issue in Singapore, despite the government's anxiousness to avoid framing national discourse in terms that highlight socio-economic inequalities among Singaporeans. That anxiousness grows out of the government's awareness of the potentially negative spillover effects of a national discourse explicitly focused on social stratification. Just as an entire generation of typists and typesetters found itself displaced by the introduction of computers, so too an entire group of Singaporeans have found themselves displaced by the skills associated with a developed economy and the forces of globalization. Structurally, there is now an underprivileged class in Singapore. It is visible in the older public housing estates, in which smaller flats and rental flats are available to those in need. Quite apart from this group, there is a group of blue collar workers with levels of skills that have deprived them of the chance fully to benefit from Singapore's growth, even as they are subjected to rising living costs. The government is well aware of this problem. It has introduced subsidized training and skill development programmes to enhance the employability of this group. To subsidize the low-wage earners it has introduced something called Workfare benefits. Determined to avoid the word "welfare", and the risks to the public purse that a welfare policy might bring, the government has introduced these benefits in the form of a payment to those whose wages fall below a certain basic amount. Similarly, employers were subsidized by the government to help them avoid layoffs during the height of the global financial crisis of the past three years.

The rise in living costs and the disproportionate manner in which certain segments of the population have benefitted from Singapore's development have certainly led to far greater levels of social stratification. Whereas some such stratification is unavoidable, it is imperative that it does not dampen the spirit of those whom it traps in a declining relative standard of living. In this regard, housing, education, and health must remain affordable, and opportunities for social mobility must continue to obtain. The mounting difficulty of access to these amenities and opportunities poses potential danger to the social fabric of the country. Importantly, the remuneration packages of public officials and high-ranking civil servants may affect their ability to empathize with the plight of Singaporeans in less affluent social strata. In its early days, PAP politicians were often cautioned by the party's leadership to exercise restraint in their consumption habits so as not to attract enmity and envy.

Some of the government's employment practices and immigration policies have led to disquiet at the ground level. This disquiet is palpable. Again, the government is well aware of the situation, and senior ministers regularly address the issue in order to allay fears. The employment practice that allows entrepreneurs to hire foreign labour without having to make contributions to the Central Provident Fund savings accounts required of Singaporeans places the latter at a significant disadvantage in some segments of the employment market. The rules governing the payment of levies for foreign workers have also been liberalized. In addition, the government has in the very recent past significantly increased Singapore's intake of immigrants and offered many immigrants permanent-resident status and citizenship. In order to promote the idea of people in both these categories as parts of a larger organic whole, the government has come recently to use the term "resident population". As a result of deliberately accelerated immigration, the current resident population in Singapore is in excess of five million persons. Foreigners account for approximately 30 per cent of the domestic resident population.

This sudden surge in the country's population has had a number of direct consequences. The first is the steep increase in property and housing prices. Another is severe strain on infrastructure and in areas like public transport and medical services. The resultant disturbances in their daily lives have led Singaporeans to take note of what they consider the negative impact of recent immigration into the city state. More importantly, there is a sense that the government ignores its own citizens and is more interested in furthering its own agenda at their significant discomfort. Deriving from this nascent sense of anger and frustration is a reduced feeling of belonging to the country and of enjoying a compact with the government. An example of the former sentiment was the opinion expressed by a national serviceman to Senior Minister Goh Chok Tong at a dialogue session that he is no longer sure of what he is fighting for. An example of the latter sentiment was the sheer disbelief of the younger domestic population that the Jemaah Islamiyah terrorist Mas Selamat Kastari had escaped from a high security detention facility in 2007. The previously successful political economy of low wages and dependence on foreign labour that deflected the domestic social costs of production and gained the PAP performance legitimacy has begun to erode. The government needs to frame a new compact in order to retain its dominance. Its own market-driven policies in important areas like housing, health, and education have also played a role in under-mining the old compact between Singapore's government and its citizens.

The enlargement of the domestic population and, through dredging and landfill, of the country's land mass derive from an old concern of the PAP's first-generation elite. The concern grew out of a reading of the history of the city states of ancient Greece that held that, unlike real countries, entities of that kind could not endure in perpetuity. That early elite and in particular current Minister Mentor Lee Kuan Yew were keen on enlarging the country and its land mass to make Singapore a more sustainable entity. During the 1980s, when the PAP's share of electoral support hovered around 60 per cent, Singapore's population challenged its government. In response, the government unveiled a series of measures to refill the country's ballast tanks — drawing on the favoured nautical analogy of the country's early leaders. It introduced the Feedback Unit in 1985 and used white papers to promote greater consultation on policy matters. It also inaugurated the Institute of Policy Studies in 1988. Today, Singapore's government seems to face the need to renew its compact with a younger generation of its citizens. How well the steely captain will deal with the seeming mutiny remains to be seen.

Rapid advances in travel and technology have left Singaporeans much better educated, more aware of their surroundings, and much better travelled. They no longer rely on the government for information and values. The battle for the hearts and minds of the younger generation is being fought in cyberspace, where the PAP lacks its traditional advantage of the control of local channels of communication and of relevant agencies. Battles will be fought differently and on more equal terms in this externally generated scenario. In the next general election, smaller Group Representation Constituencies and more single-member wards will open up more competitive opportunities for the political opposition. The debut of the Reform Party and a potential alliance between that party's Kenneth Jeyaratnam and Chiam See Tong of the Singapore People's Party and Singapore Democratic Alliance are also worth watching. The election, due by early 2012 but widely expected to be called far sooner, is also likely to be Lee Kuan Yew's last. It may well be worth noting that no politician after him will ever match the legitimacy that he enjoys. The PAP will have to learn to bear with the range of consequences that will arise from all the changes to the Singapore scenario that the near future will bring.

Thailand

Matthew Wheeler

The consequences of the 2006 *coup d'état* that ousted Prime Minister Thaksin Shinawatra will continue to reverberate in Thailand during 2011. The *coup d'état* served as the *coup de grâce* for a consensus, embodied in the 1997 Constitution, on how political power should be gained and exercised. Thaksin's creeping authoritarianism, and the challenge to Thailand's oligarchy implicit in his party's electoral successes, undermined this consensus; the consensus unraveled completely as defenders of the traditional social order reacted with anachronistic, unconstitutional military intervention. The result has been a protracted and sometimes violent political crisis, unfolding amid growing anxiety about royal succession as the end of King Bhumipol Adulyadej's six-decade reign draws nearer. In short, Thai politics is now playing out in the absence of a consensus on the very basis of legitimacy itself.

In 2011, Thailand will face a moment of truth. Prime Minister Abhisit Vejjajiva, leader of the Democrat Party (DP), must dissolve Parliament and schedule an election by the end of the parliamentary term in December. The significance of the general election will register beyond the level of conventional politics. While the election may be expected to determine who will govern, more revealing of Thailand's political trajectory will be whether or not the election results are honoured. Is the ballot box an effective means of making political claims? Is the political process capable of regulating social conflict? Can the voters be trusted? Answers to these questions will portend the future of the Thai polity.

In 2010, the contest between proponents of the status quo — represented by elements of the military, bureaucracy, palace, and Democrat Party — and forces aligned with or sympathetic to Thaksin, including the United Front for Democracy Against Dictatorship (UDD) and the Puea Thai Party (PTP), escalated into violence. Beginning in mid-March, red-shirted UDD protesters took to Bangkok's streets demanding a fresh election. After two months of protests that shut down what is in effect contemporary Bangkok's centre, units of the

THAILAND

Land Area:	514,000 sq. km.
Population (2009 World Bank data):	67,764,033
Capital:	Bangkok
Type of Government:	Parliamentary democracy and constitutional monarchy
Head of State:	King Bhumibol Adulyadej
Head of Government:	Prime Minister Abhisit Vejjajiva
Last Election:	2007
Next Election Due:	2011
Currency Used:	Thai Baht
US$ Exchange Rate (2 December 2010):	US$1 = 30 baht

Thai Army encircled the Ratchaprasong Intersection protest site and battled with red-shirt supporters for six days. On 19 May, troops pushed into the UDD encampment, dispersing the protesters and sparking arson attacks not only across Bangkok but also in up-country Thailand. The Democrat-led coalition survived, but at a price: 91 dead, including 11 members of the security forces, and more than 2,000 injured in clashes from 10 April to 19 May.

The government's response to the unrest — according to official statistics, the most deadly episode of political violence in modern Thai history — has been equivocal, emphasizing national reconciliation while vigorously suppressing dissent. Abhisit impanelled high-level commissions to study social and political reform, but these commissions lack opposition voices. And they will not deliver their recommendations until 2012. Meanwhile, the Center for the Resolution of the Emergency Situation (CRES), a military-dominated agency established in 2009 to coordinate government responses to red-shirt protests, has pursued a determined crackdown on opposition activists. The CRES closed down opposition publications and radio stations, blocked tens of thousands of websites, and detained hundreds of government critics without charge under provisions of the Thaksin-era Emergency Decree. The government has accused its opponents, including the opposition PTP, of plotting to topple the monarchy. *Lèse majesté* cases have been brought with unprecedented frequency, and sentences have become harsher.

Events in 2010 brought no resolution to the conflict that has roiled Thailand for the past five years. Certain features of the political environment may be expected to persist in 2011: simmering red-shirt anger at perceived legal and judicial double standards; low-level terrorism that lends substance to fears of incipient red-shirt armed resistance; demonization of government opponents as enemies of the monarchy; suppression of dissent through censorship, arrests, and intimidation; resolute opposition by the military leadership to resurgent "Thaksinism"; and continued political and social polarization. Insurgency in the Malay-Muslim-majority southernmost provinces will fester, its solution awaiting resolution of the national-level conflict.

Parties and factions have been preparing for an election that, many observers anticipate, will come before mid-year. The military-backed 2007 Constitution weakened the executive and enhanced the leverage of small parties and factions, setting the stage for a return to fractious coalition governments, horse trading, and vote buying. Thailand's next election is likely to see revival of the old-style money politics that Thaksin's dominance made largely redundant. The military and bureaucracy may be expected to pull out all the stops to influence the election, using security laws and state-owned media against the opposition. Results of a general election are likely to be close.

At time of writing, the DP faces dissolution and a ban on its executives in separate cases of misusing campaign funds and accepting illegal donations. A Constitutional Court ruling against the DP could quiet charges of double standards, and the party could be reconstituted under a new name. Secretly recorded videos posted on the Internet, apparently showing a Democrat Member of Parliament attempting to influence judges and unethical behaviour by court officials, have cast doubt on the court's impartiality.

In spite of these legal challenges, the DP (or its successor) can campaign on sound management of the economy and introduction of social welfare measures including debt relief for farmers and free schooling. These programmes are not likely to help the DP in the vote-rich Thaksin stronghold of the Northeast, where the DP must rely on the scandal-plagued Bhumjai Thai Party to compete with the PTP. Bhumjai Thai controls the Ministry of Interior and will expect handpicked governors and district officials to deliver votes. Notwithstanding establishment claims to disdain the venality of politics, money to entice factions and voters may represent the best hope for status quo forces to retain control of government. The PTP, meanwhile, must struggle to overcome weak leadership. It will attempt to exploit the legacy of the April–May 2010 crackdown and highlight alleged government corruption.

Thailand's predicament is that a general election may not bring stability. If an election produces another DP-led coalition, red shirts and their sympathizers are likely to question the fairness of the process. They are also sure to challenge the government in the streets. A PTP victory would likewise prompt a reaction. Thaksin-aligned parties have prevailed in every general election since 2001. Status quo forces have taken extraordinary measures to reverse these outcomes since 2006, including the coup, the occupation of Government House and Bangkok's airports by the yellow-shirted People's Alliance for Democracy in 2008, and court rulings that ousted two consecutive prime ministers. It is widely assumed that the powers-that-be have deemed such measures necessary to ensure that a compliant government holds office during the dreaded but inevitable period of royal succession. There is no sign that these forces are prepared to abide an outcome that does not accord with their preferences. Given a close result, the Election Commission and the courts could chip away at a PTP majority by disqualifying its candidates for various infractions. The army could intervene, applying pressure to broker a coalition as it did in 2008 or seizing power to "reset" the political situation.

A general election could be cancelled or postponed. Thailand's establishment will have to determine if the costs of postponing an election, such as increased voter anger and international opprobrium, are greater than the costs of reversing an undesirable electoral outcome. If the latter costs weigh more heavily, a security-related pretext could suffice. Prime Minister Abhisit has cautioned that dissolution of Parliament and ensuing elections are conditional on a peaceful environment. One election commissioner went so far as to suggest that it would be better to amend the constitution to extend the term of the current government to ten years rather than to hold an election under turbulent conditions.

There remains some, very limited, scope for an elite compromise that could balance the interests of the establishment with those of the Thaksin camp. But the basis of such a compromise is not evident, and the conflict appears to remain a zero-sum game. Senior officials, including army chief General Prayuth Chanocha, have cast the conflict in the starkest terms, as one between "Thainess" and republicanism. PTP leaders have proclaimed their intention to bring Thaksin back should they regain power. Such a move would certainly provoke the military's royalists. Moreover, it is by no means assured that an elite-level compromise would appease rank-and-file partisans on either side.

Moves to delay an election or to reverse the results of polls carry the risk of alienating uncommitted Thais and convincing red shirts that the political order is irredeemable. Hundreds of thousands of Thais have taken to the streets to press political claims over the past six years. They have done so peacefully, for the most part, but protests have also included incidents of criminality and deadly violence. Further mass demonstrations must be anticipated, especially if an election is postponed or in effect nullified. Renewed red-shirt protests in the latter half of 2010 illustrated a continued readiness to take risks and to flout the Emergency Decree still in force in Bangkok. A spate of bombings hint at a revolutionary direct-action alternative.

The process of achieving a new consensus on political legitimacy in Thailand will be long, complex, and difficult. Under current circumstances a general election cannot bridge Thailand's socio-political divide. By the same token, most Thais are unlikely to consent to a formula for legitimacy that scorns the principle of respect for majority preferences.

Vietnam

David Koh

Regional Outlook 2010–2011 argued that the 2011 National Congress of the Communist Party of Vietnam (CPV) would prove the defining event for all political developments in the country during the five years thereafter. As the deadline for contributions to *Regional Outlook 2011–2012* arrived, the politics of the Party Congress began to heat up. Blame for the bankruptcy of the state shipping conglomerate Vinashin was placed alternately on the Vietnamese political system itself and on the shoulders of the Prime Minister and his Cabinet; it depended on whose supporters one talked to. A number of provincial party leaders were fired for bad behaviour and wrongdoing, and party congresses at the provincial level and in such important sectors as the military and public security concluded. The competition for top posts below the national level was over by late 2010. During 2011–12, the most important event in Vietnam would be the Party Congress itself, due about a month before Lunar New Year (Tet) 2011.

As no CPV General Secretary can serve more than two terms and as the term now coming to an end was Nong Duc Manh's second, the spring in 2011 will see the party welcome a new leader. The process of selection for General Secretary is top-down, and the General Secretary–designate will come from the current members of the CPV Political Bureau. More than that, at the top the process is consensual, and decided ultimately by voting within the Political Bureau. The successor must be anointed by most of those senior figures whose opinions matter, a group that includes the Political Bureau, retired leaders who still wield influence, and members of the CPV Central Committee to be elected at the approaching National Party Congress. A small minority of party members have called for the direct election of the General Secretary by the National Party Congress, delegates to which will number more than 1,000. As the fifteen-member Political Bureau and 150-member central committee would have to agree to such a change, and as its legal basis would require the amendment of CPV statutes, its is unlikely to happen any time soon.

VIETNAM

Land Area:	332,000 sq. km.
Population (2009 World Bank data):	87,279,754
Capital:	Hanoi
Type of Government:	Socialist republic
Head of State:	President Nguyen Minh Triet
General Secretary of the Communist Party of Vietnam:	Nong Duc Manh
Head of Government:	Prime Minister Nguyen Tan Dung
Last Election:	2007
Next Election:	2011
Currency Used:	Dong
US$ Exchange Rate (2 December 2010):	US$1 = 19,495 dong

At time of writing a majority of decision-makers appeared to favour either Prime Minister Nguyen Tan Dung, the third-ranking member of the Political Bureau, or Nguyen Phu Trong, Chairman of the National Assembly during 2006–11 and currently the fourth-ranking member of the Political Bureau, as the next General Secretary of the CPV. Standing Secretary Truong Tan Sang, effectively deputy general secretary and fifth-ranking in political power, would have a good chance if either of the former candidates came to be seen as unelectable by the incoming Party Central Committee.

How would either or both of these two men become unelectable, between now and the Party Congress in late January 2011? Make no mistake about it: the CPV will protect them from any direct link to serious problems during this period. But they could be indirectly affected by corruption and mismanagement scandals occurring in areas for which their supporters have responsibility, an outcome which would suggest the incompetence and irresponsibility of the patron.

The weight of Vinashin's problems has hung around Prime Minister Nguyen Tan Dung's neck, even though the Political Bureau technically absolved him of responsibility. Observers believe that the exposure of Vinashin's bankruptcy so close to the CPV National Congress was a political attack on the Prime Minister, intended to influence opinion within the central committee and to turn its members' votes against him. This attack came even though the Political Bureau had publicly declared that fault for the bankruptcy was not the Prime Minister's alone. Indeed, just after the Vinashin case broke, Hanoi was full of talk that Nguyen Tan Dung could surely not weather it and continue for another term in office. In his favour, however, is his record of having overseen five years of economic growth in a climate of global instability.

The chief weakness in Nguyen Phu Trong's candidacy to become CPV General Secretary is not securing an ideological breakthrough in the application of Marxism-Leninism to Vietnam. In preparation for the 2011 Party Congress, Trong oversaw the first revision of the Party Manifesto since 1991. His critics voice disappointment that the revised manifesto retains the idea that state ownership is central to the stewardship of the Vietnamese economy, even as the country's state-owned enterprises are arguably a severe drain on both the state budget and national productivity. Trong's supporters argue that he has the ability to strike a balance among different policy demands, as every top leader should. They contend that a steady hand like his would be useful in an unstable geostrategic climate — a reference to the turbulence of the South China Sea issue and to the growing intensity of great-power politics in East Asia.

Ultimately Vietnam's choice of a new leadership will be based on these sorts of discourse among the CPV elites responsible for making that choice. If the discourse emphasizes the need for stability, the choice of someone whose views seem close to the CPV's ideology and who has the ability easily to strike consensus within the Party will be logical. Nguyen Phu Tong is supposedly such a person. But if the discourse turned towards the need for quick and decisive reforms to move Vietnam forward in double-quick tempo, than Nguyen Tan Dung is the favourite. If there is no consensus, a third person might get the job. The Party Central Committee Plenum of late November–early December 2011 will have offered indications of the direction of this debate and its ultimate outcome.

The National Assembly election, likely to be held in May 2011, will have less importance than the coming CPV Party Congress. The current National Assembly agreed to the shortening of its term from five to four years so that elections to the new assembly could follow closely upon the CPV's National Party Congress. The rationale is that this timetable will allow the CPV's new leadership to see to the new assembly's promptly selecting a new Prime Minister and government. All Vietnamese ministers are top CPV Central Committee and/or Political Bureau members; they must be elected members of the National Assembly in order to become ministers.

The National Assembly now has specialized commissions responsible for scrutinizing government policy. Criticism of policy emanating from the assembly has become increasingly high-profile and direct; it has also been reported in Vietnam's lively mass media. In 2011, however, the National Assembly is likely to have only one full sitting to scrutinize government policy, at the end of the year. As new members will have first to find their footing, the levels of interaction and scrutiny might be toned down a notch early in the term of the next National Assembly.

In the realm of foreign policy, Vietnam will no longer hold the chairmanship of the ASEAN Standing Committee in 2011. After a strong showing in 2010, however, it will proudly pass the baton to Indonesia. Its major achievements during the year included bringing the South China Sea issue back to the world's attention and above all to the attention of the United States, staging a meeting of the ASEAN Defence Ministers Meeting Plus, and the expansion of the East Asian Summit to include the United States and Russia. As regards the South China Sea, Vietnam must still win other ASEAN member states' agreement to a U.S. role in resolving the issue.

What can we look forward to in 2011 and 2012? Vietnam is very much interested in turning the Declaration on Conduct in the South China Sea into a Code of Conduct, and apparently this wish has found some support, including a voice or two from China. We should expect Vietnam to work towards this goal. Other foreign policy goals include the continued bilateral engagement of the great powers; additional economic and business agreements with the United States, China, Japan, and Europe are a priority. Vietnam will also continue to work to engage each of the permanent members of the United Nations Security Council on a stronger and more sustainable basis. The great powers have indirectly recognized that Vietnam will become a much more important player than it is now — at least in the challenging geopolitics of East Asia. Everybody will be paying more attention to Vietnam and to winning its friendship in the Great East Asian Game.

Economic Outlook

REGIONAL ECONOMIC OUTLOOK

Sanchita Basu Das

Southeast Asia's GDP growth is almost back on stream after an uncertain 2008 and 2009. First-half GDP growth has been better than most expected. Singapore posted a spectacular 18.1 per cent year-on-year (y/y) growth in the first half of 2010, while Indonesia accelerated at 6 per cent and Malaysia at 9.5 per cent over the same period. The recovery was mainly driven by resurgent exports in the manufacturing sector and increase in domestic demand. The resulting increase in manufacturing output led to firming up of labour markets and higher wages, which in turn supported higher private consumption.

Capital inflows have also rapidly returned to the region. This is in terms of both direct investment and portfolio flows. Vietnam posted higher foreign direct investment (FDI) disbursement in the first half of 2010 to US$5.4 billion, up nearly 6 per cent over the same period last year. Despite unsettled political affairs in Thailand, the number of foreign investment projects during January–March 2010 soared by 30.5 per cent to 184 from 141 in the same quarter the year before.

REGIONAL ECONOMIC OUTLOOK

- Growth in Southeast Asia is expected to slow down in 2011 and 2012 after a strong performance in 2010.

- Aggregate inflation will continue to rise in the next two years.

- Current account surplus (as a percentage of GDP) for the region will narrow on higher imports.

- Downside risks from the advanced economies will persist.

Foreign portfolio investment has also surged, especially into Indonesia and Thailand, driven by profitable trades in the equity and fixed income markets.

The stock market rallied on the improved economic outlook and revival in capital inflows (Figure 1). The Singapore stock exchange jumped 15 per cent by October from the beginning of 2010. Indonesia's stock market, Jakarta Composite Index, swelled more than 39 per cent since January 2010. The surge in capital inflows caused exchange rates to appreciate strongly. The Philippines peso and Malaysian ringgit strengthened more than 7.2 per cent and 9.1 per cent since the start of the year (Figure 2). While the monetary authorities in the region are intervening in exchange markets, it appears to have had limited success in stemming the appreciation thus far.

Figure 1. Relative Performance of ASEAN-5 Main Stock Market Indices, 2007–2010

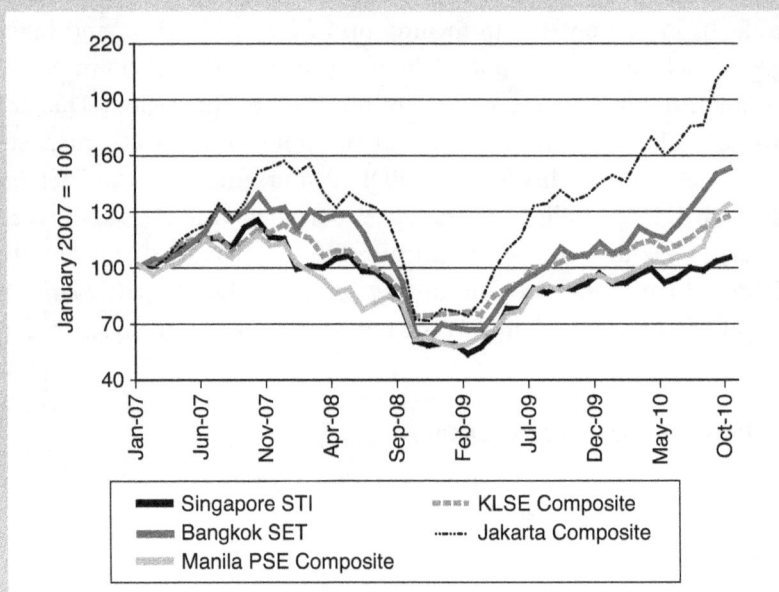

Singapore STI
Bangkok SET
Manila PSE Composite
KLSE Composite
Jakarta Composite

SOURCE: Bloomberg.

Figure 2. Relative Performance of ASEAN-5 Currencies to the U.S. Dollar, 2007–2010

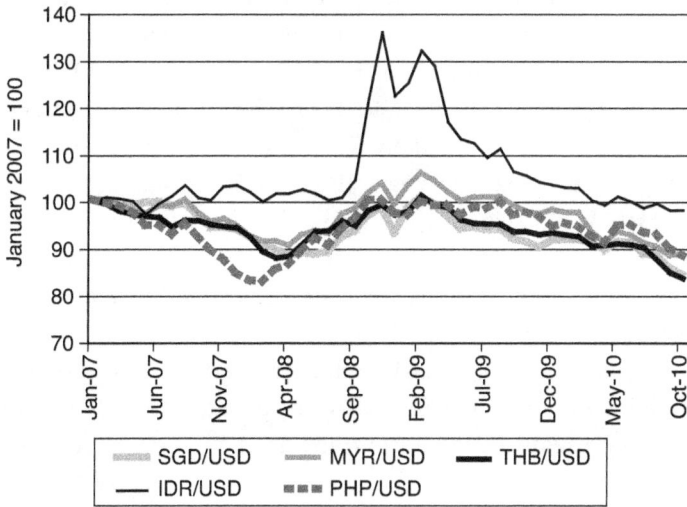

However, this exceptionally strong performance in the first half of 2010 is unlikely to be sustained for the rest of 2010 and 2011. This is because, first, the high base effect of GDP growth in the second half of 2009 will come into play. Second, with recovery appearing to be firmly on track, fiscal and monetary authorities are likely to complete the gradual unwinding of policy stimulus in 2011. Interest rates have already been raised in Malaysia, Thailand, and Vietnam, and other measures have been taken to contain emerging asset bubbles in some stock and property markets. Third, with weakness in major trading partners (Japan, the United States, and the European Union), Southeast Asia will also experience low economic activity across the region.

Given this, economic growth in the Southeast Asian region is expected to slow to 5.4 per cent in 2011 compared to 7.4 per cent in 2010 (ADB 2010). While Malaysia, Singapore, Thailand, and the

Philippines are expected to contract, Indonesia, Cambodia, and Vietnam will probably expand in the range of 6–7 per cent. For Indonesia, the government will likely implement the major policies formulated in the National Medium-Term Development Plan, which targets raising average annual GDP growth to 6.3–6.8 per cent in 2010–14, and lowering the poverty incidence to 8–10 per cent. For Malaysia, its tenth development plan is likely to boost domestic investment and fuel growth in the next few years (Figures 3 and 4).

Southeast Asia's strong upswing is causing inflationary pressures. Consumer prices have trended higher since third-quarter 2009 largely due to the rise in global commodity prices and private transport costs. Aggregate inflation will continue to rise and will average around 4.2 per cent y/y in 2011 on narrowing output gap. In 2011, planned reduction in subsidies in some economies will further add to inflationary pressures. The central banks in several economies of

Figure 3. Real GDP Growth in the ASEAN-5 Countries, 2006–2012F

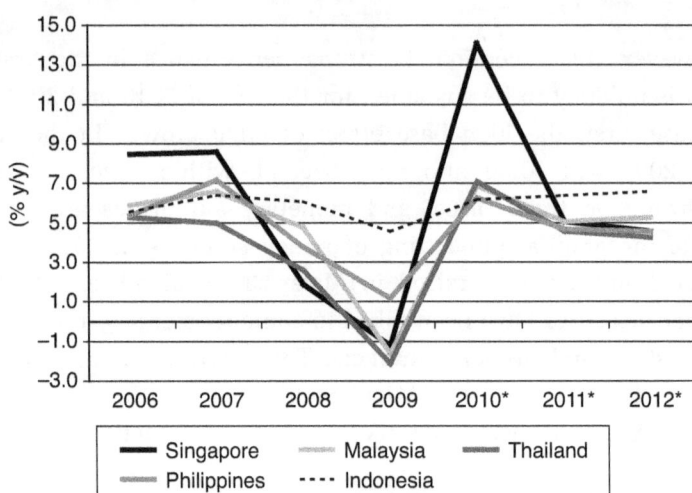

NOTE: * 2010, 2011, and 2012 are estimated GDP growth rates.
SOURCE: ADB, World Bank, author's estimate.

Figure 4. Real GDP Growth in Brunei, Cambodia, Laos, Vietnam, and Southeast Asia, 2006–2012F

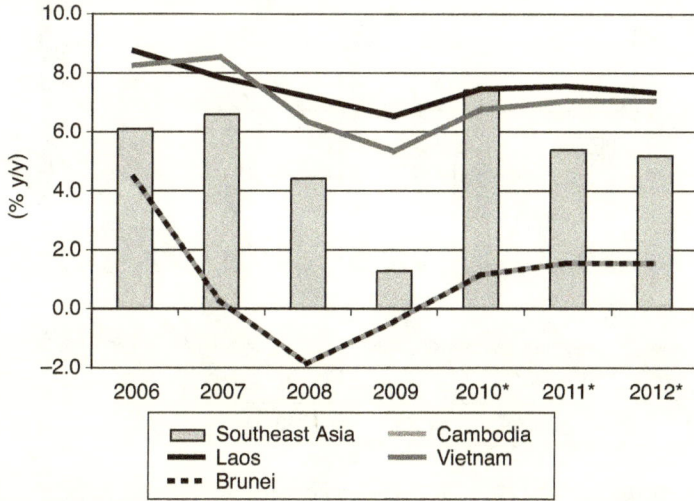

NOTE: * 2010, 2011, and 2012 are estimated GDP growth rates.
SOURCE: ADB and author's estimate.

the region (Malaysia, Thailand, and the Philippines) are implementing measures for a subdued inflation. For other economies, like Singapore and Indonesia, a steady appreciation of the currency against the U.S. dollar is helping to contain the imported inflation (Figure 5).

Rapid economic recovery has been aided by a significant improvement in the external sector of the region. After contracting for the most of 2009, exports posted a strong growth in the first half of 2010. However, going ahead, export growth is likely to moderate owing to a less supportive global environment and the completion of inventory building exercises in most of the industrial economies. Import growth is likely to remain robust as a result of buoyant domestic demand. Consequently, the overall current account surplus as a share of GDP is expected to decline to 5.7 per cent in 2010 and 2011 from 7.1 per cent in 2009 (Figure 6).

Figure 5. Inflation Rate in Southeast Asian Economies, 2009–2012F

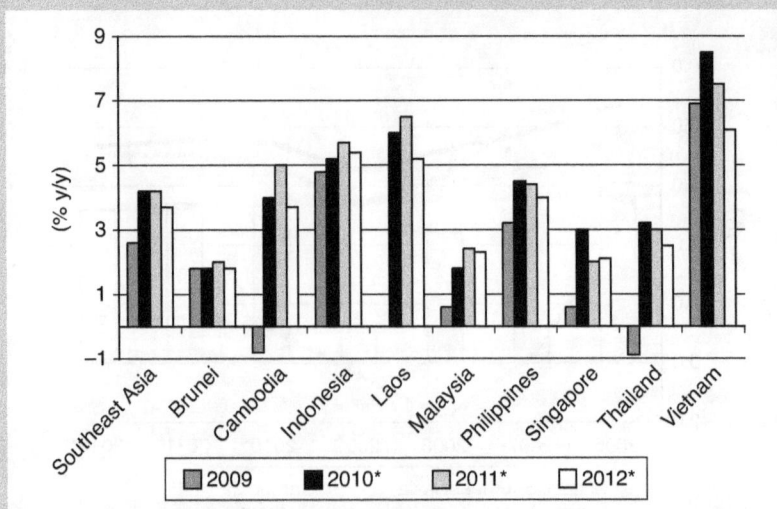

NOTE: *2010, 2011, and 2012 are estimated inflation.
SOURCE: ADB, IMF and author's estimate.

Figure 6. Current Account Balance in Southeast Asian Economies, 2009–2012F

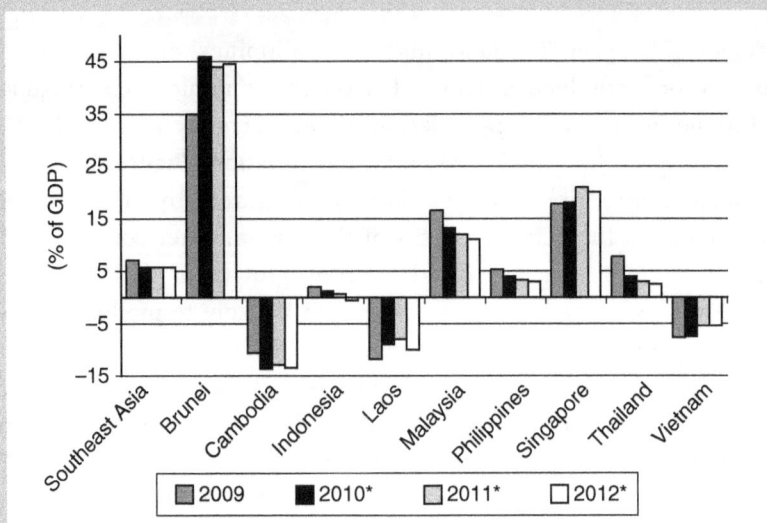

NOTE: *2010, 2011, and 2012 are estimated figures.
SOURCE: ADB and author's estimate.

On the whole, managing recovery in Southeast Asia is proving to be just as challenging as managing the crisis. The policymakers are facing two sets of challenges that they need to efficiently balance. First, the region is experiencing faster-than-expected economic recovery that is causing overheating in a few sectors. Singapore, for example, is facing a sharp spike in real estate prices while Thailand is trying for a subdued inflation that is increasingly becoming demand-side driven. Also, rapid growth and rising interest rate differentials is resulting in large capital inflows. This is leading to currency appreciation and central banks intervention, though seemingly with limited success. Indonesia has also resorted to capital controls (e.g., imposing a one-month holding period for central bank debt, introducing instruments for investors to park money longer term) to check the destabilizing effect of the huge foreign capital inflows.

Second, the policymakers are worried about the sustainability of the recent growth pattern. While many of the region's economies performed better than expected, this rebound was partly attributed to inventory restocking from a weak base in 2009. This is likely to moderate in the second half of 2010 and 2011. The region also remains vulnerable to the European and the U.S. markets. Any further disturbance in these advanced economies will definitely undermine the growth recovery. This is especially because the advanced economies' policy discretion to deal with further shocks has diminished and China, the main growth engine for the Southeast Asian economies, also depends on advanced markets for the final export demand. So downside risks from advanced economies persist.

REFERENCES

Asian Development Bank (ADB). *Asian Development Outlook 2010 Update: The Future of Growth in Asia*. Manila: ADB, 2010.

International Monetary Fund (IMF). *World Economic Outlook: Recovery, Risk, and Rebalancing*. Washington, DC: IMF, 2010.

World Bank. *World Bank East Asia and Pacific Economic Update 2010, Volume 2*. Washington, DC: World Bank, 2010.

SECOND-TIER CITIES IN SOUTHEAST ASIA

Francis E. Hutchinson

Far away from the seats of economic and political power, secondary urban centres in Southeast Asia are seeing an unusual amount of activity. Cebu and Davao in the Philippines are becoming important business-process outsourcing centres. In Malaysia, Penang and Johor Bahru are consolidating their positions in manufacturing, with important investments in the medical device and petrochemical sectors, respectively. In Indonesia, Surabaya and other cities such as Makassar and Balikpapan are benefiting from high commodity prices.

This dynamism in secondary urban centres is something new for Southeast Asia. Home to megacities such as Manila, Bangkok, Jakarta and — to a lesser extent — Kuala Lumpur, the region has been characterized by the disproportionate concentration of economic activity in capitals. This reaches extremes in the Philippines and Thailand, where Manila and Bangkok each account for more than half of total gross domestic product (Rimmer and Dick 2009).

In contrast to North America and Europe, where industrialization was accompanied by the emergence of new and larger urban centres, Southeast Asia had a limited number of large urban centres when it began industrializing. Economies of scale accompanied by economic nationalism, political centralization, and the establishment of customs procedures and trade barriers led to the concentration of commerce and industry in capital cities. By the 1970s, influential secondary cities such as Surabaya, Cebu, Chiang Mai, and Penang were shadows of their former selves (Rimmer and Dick 2009).

In the long run, it is hard for secondary cities to compete with capital cities for government resources and private investment. In addition to the capitals' proximity to decision-makers, primary urban centres also have privileged access to high-end infrastructure such as airports, stock exchanges, and financial institutions. Thus, in order to attract investment, second tier cities must outperform the capital as well as other contending cities.

This new, more dispersed dynamism could parallel developments in China and India, where second tier cities are emerging as a new frontier. On one hand, evolving technology and organizational processes mean that production processes can be divided up and relocated to a wider range of sites. On the other, internal dynamics in these countries are leading firms to question established business strategies focused on primary cities and look to other urban areas for untapped markets and new production sites (Boston Consulting 2010).

There are several "push" and "pull" factors driving these developments. From the push side, it is clear that Southeast Asian commercial capitals are suffering from diseconomies of scale. Clogged infrastructure, rising real estate prices, increasing pollution, and, in many cases, saturated markets have made everyday business operations more complex in Manila, Bangkok, Jakarta, and Kuala Lumpur (Spire Research and Consulting 2010). These issues can be critical during the growth phase for new sectors. For example, India's software sector started in Mumbai, but subsequently migrated to other, less-congested cities.

From the pull side, the number of cities that can constitute substantial markets or host operations is rising. Sustained economic expansion, population growth, and increasing urbanization entail a wider range of potential sites or untapped markets. The Philippines and Malaysia have more than 60 per cent of their populations living in urban areas, and Indonesia's urbanization rate is above 40 per cent. Thailand, for its part, is less urbanized, with only a third of its population living in cities (ADB 2010). Overall, this translates into a growing number of cities throughout these countries — Indonesia and even Thailand have at least five secondary cities with populations above one million (Spire Research and Consulting 2010).

In addition to having growing numbers of urban consumers, some of these cities constitute attractive production sites. For example, Bandung in Indonesia has sixteen universities and more than forty professional institutes, which could be tapped by skill-intensive operations. Cebu, Clark, and Davao in the Philippines are drawing away business process outsourcing activities from Manila, leveraging their own education systems and lower operational costs. Other urban centres are interesting because of their proximity to specific commodities. Johor Bahru in Malaysia is an important site for the processing and storage of palm oil, as is Balikpapan for oil, gas, and timber.

Accessing these attributes has been made easier through decentralization measures, which means that provincial and local authorities are now the main points of contact for investors, as opposed to central government agencies in far away capital cities. Changed incentive structures as well as greater competition for investment mean that authorities in lesser-known areas are also more proactive, with many offering individualized liaison services and

SECOND-TIER CITIES IN SOUTHEAST ASIA (continued)

attractive incentive packages. In some cases, such as Indonesia, they also have more money to spend, thanks to greater transfers of funds from central governments.

However, while this scenario offers new markets, less burdened infrastructure, untapped pools of skilled labour, and more amenable government officials, it is not without challenges.

From the marketing side, accessing this more diverse population requires a deeper knowledge of local tastes, consumption habits, and buying patterns. Secondary cities are not uniform urban centres. Rather, they have different characteristics, depending on their economic structures, geographic location, and relationship with surrounding cities. Some cities are trade hubs for surrounding urban areas, others are dependent on a specific commodity or industry, and others are less connected to the modern economy. Accessing each of these different types of city will require distinct strategies (Boston Consulting 2010).

From the production side, while basic infrastructure may be less burdened, second tier cities may also have less high-end transport and communications facilities. Airports with international connections, ports with substantial handling capacity, and a diversified base of logistics providers may well be out of reach. In addition, a dearth of experienced and reliable construction firms may make building specialist facilities impossible.

Next, while second tier cities can offer qualified and cost-effective labour, their smaller talent pools may be depleted by a large investment or unable to scale up when needed. For the same reason, highly specialized skills may be difficult to come by. Human resource intensive sectors also rely on an array of supporting services such as recruitment agencies, training institutes, and accreditation bodies — all of which may be lacking off the beaten track.

It may also be difficult to entice senior and middle management to relocate to second tier cities. Both national and international staff may be reluctant to deal with a different local language and more basic education, health, and recreation facilities. Conversely, less pollution and traffic may tip the scale in the other direction.

Finally, while local government officials in these areas may be all too eager to attract investment, there may still be a substantial learning process for both industry players and policymakers. Bureaucratic capacity, linguistic abilities, and even knowledge of national government policies may lag behind that of first tier city administrations. Useful lobby groups such as business associations may also be underdeveloped.

The economic geography of Southeast Asia is slowly being redrawn. While large, capital cities will rule for the foreseeable future, secondary urban centres are likely to garner significant attention as new untapped markets, as well as less congested sites for production.

References

Asian Development Bank. *Key Indicators for Asia and the Pacific*. Manila: Asian Development Bank, 2010.

Boston Consulting Group. "Winning in Emerging-market Cities: A Guide to the World's Largest Growth Opportunity", 2010.

Rimmer, Peter J. and Howard Dick. *The City in Southeast Asia: Patterns, Process and Policy*. Singapore: NUS Press, 2009.

Spire Research and Consulting. "The Next Frontier in Asia: How Asia's Second-tier Cities are the World's New Marketing Arena", 2010.

SINGAPORE AND THE INTEGRATED RESORTS
Sanchita Basu Das

The year 2010 witnessed the opening of two integrated resorts (IRs) — Marina Bay Sands (MBS) and Resorts World at Sentosa (RWS) — in Singapore. This is part of Singapore policymaker's efforts not only to adjust themselves to the changing global landscape but also to broaden the structure of the economy. It is also the initial part of a larger government plan to raise tourism receipts to SG$30 billion (from SG$12.8 billion in 2009) and double visitor arrivals to 17 million by 2015.

Why Integrated Resorts? Singapore has always been adapting to the dynamic economic environment and reinventing itself by adding new engines of economic growth. It observed three major changes in the region:

1. Tourism trends: In 1991, a tourist used to spend on average four days in Singapore but that came down to three days during 2002–04. On the other hand, they were spending on average about four days in Hong Kong. To gain competitiveness in the tourism industry, Singapore has to invest in the tourism sector. IRs served as a way to this objective. Developing IRs in the city state will have spillover effects on other industries — hotel, food and beverage, retail, transport etc.

2. Major cities elsewhere had also been undergoing makeovers since early 2000. In Asia, Hong Kong opened its Disneyland in 2005 and Malaysia developed its Kuala Lumpur City Centre (KLCC) project.

3. The past few years saw the rise of the middle class in India, China, and other Southeast Asian nations. Asia is forecast to account for 43 per cent of worldwide consumption by 2030. This group of people tends to spend more on tourism than earlier. Again, tourism is bound to increase by the emergence of budget airlines in the region.

What was expected from the setting up of the IRs? IRs were forecast to contribute to growth in two ways: First, they were expected to benefit the economy from the investment and construction spending. For example, as at 31 December 2009, RWS' investment in the IR stood at SG$6.6 billion. It spent SG$826 million on construction work and other property, plant, and equipment during the six months to 30 June 2010. These represent significant value addition to Singapore's GDP. Second, IRs were expected to draw in more tourists and support the services industry of the island economy. It was expected to benefit Singapore's job market and add on to government coffers.

Keeping these in mind, in 2006, according to the Ministry of Trade and Industry (MTI), it was estimated that MBS and RWS could each generate about SG$2.7 billion of value-add or about 0.8 per cent of Singapore's GDP by 2015. Again, in January 2010, the Minister of Trade and Industry, Lim Hng Kiang revealed that the two IRs are estimated to bring in 0.5–1 per cent of Singapore's GDP when fully operational. Private sector estimates have ranged from between 0.3 per cent to 1.8 per cent of GDP.

So how are the IRs contributing to the economy? During 2008–09, the Singapore economy benefitted from the construction phase of the IRs. This was especially during the global economic crisis, when most of the sectors were struggling to maintain a positive growth rate in the economy. In that phase, the construction sector was supported by the building of the two IRs — MBS, which features a 2,500-room hotel, casino, and theatre; and RWS, which comprises six hotels with a total of 1,800 rooms, a casino, and an entertainment complex, Universal Studios Singapore. The construction phase of the IRs also lifted demand for construction workers that added to the resiliency of the labour market compared to the previous crises in Singapore.

In 2010, during the first nine months, the tourist arrivals in the country have been rising (Figure 1). Tourist arrivals rose to a whopping one million visitors in July, the highest number the city state had ever seen in a month. Consequently, the hotel industry became a big beneficiary. According to the Singapore Tourism Board, in the first half of 2010, the average room rate was SG$204, compared with SG$195 over the same period the previous year. The hotel occupancy rate was also higher at 85 per cent in the first six months of 2010 vis-à-vis 72 per cent in 2009. While the low base effect and strong recovery in Asia may have helped, the two IRs have also played a significant role.

Looking at the GDP statistics, according to the MTI, the economy expanded by 18.8 per cent and the services sector by 11.2 per cent in the second quarter of 2010 from a year ago. Of this, the "other services" category showed a major change since the beginning of 2010. In the past, the long-term growth rate of this sector has been almost stable around 4.5 per cent. However, the "other services" sector showed a much higher growth rate of 7.4 and 13 per cent in Q1 and Q2 respectively (Figure 2). In absolute terms, "other services" was worth SG$13.2 billion in the first half of the year, compared to SG$11.9 billion the same period last year. This jump in "other services" was caused largely due to the IRs.

SINGAPORE AND THE INTEGRATED RESORTS (continued)

Figure 1. Tourist Arrivals in Singapore

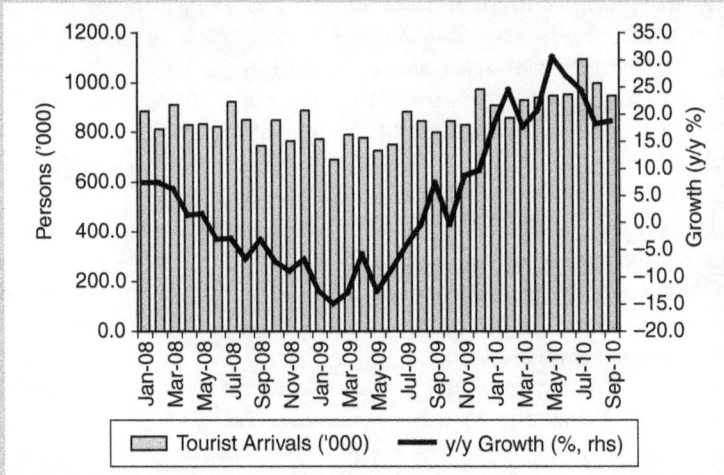

SOURCE: CEIC Database.

Figure 2. Significant Growth in "Other Sevices" Category

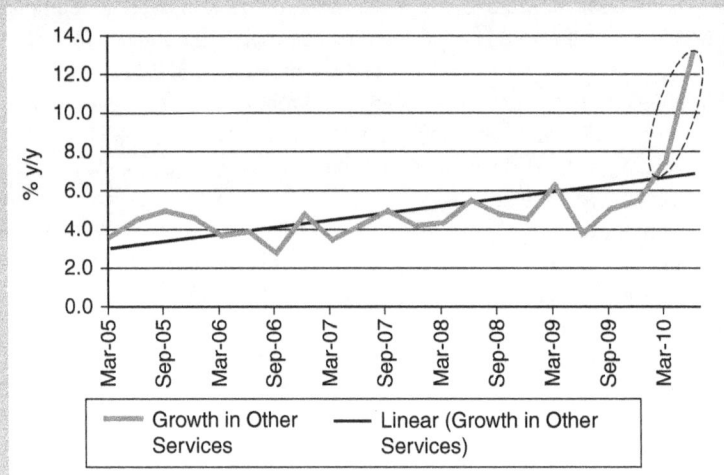

SOURCE: CEIC Database.

For more accurate estimation of the IRs contribution to total GDP, reports reveal that the RWS and MBS added SG$470 million to Singapore's economy or about 0.3 percentage points to GDP in the first half of the year (DBS Group Research 2010). But it must be noted that both the resorts were not fully operational during the review period. While RWS commenced operations only by the end of January, MBS came into operation only in late April. The two IRs are expected to contribute SG$2 billion or 0.7 percentage points to the full-year GDP growth.

Besides the economic gains mentioned above, the IRs also generate economic spin-offs that benefit retail, hospitality, conventions and exhibitions, food and beverage industries, and logistics industry as well. They also complement the other boosters to the economy like the Youth Olympic Games, Formula 1, etc. Thus, the overall contribution to the economy is likely to be much larger.

That said, it may be a bit early to get a clear picture of the IRs' contribution to the Singapore economy. Nevertheless, the opening up of the two IRs in 2010 validates the policymakers approach to pragmatism and flexibility. While the government initially resisted casinos in the city state, they amended the policy in 2005, which, looking back, came at the right time before the global financial crisis. Now with the economic recovery on track, the two IRs are expected to bring in 17 million tourists within five years who will spend in excess of SG$30 billion and help create over 100,000 jobs, directly and indirectly. Indeed, the two iconic attractions are going to help Singapore in sustaining its position as an attractive destination for foreign enterprises, investors, tourists, and talents.

References

Chan, Robin. "Counting the IR chips". *Straits Times*, 26 August 2010.

DBS Group Research. "Singapore: GDP Contributions of the IRs", August 2010.

Jha, Jyoti. "Singapore's New Economic Engines Boosting Growth Rate". *Business Climate*, September 2010.

Ministry of Trade and Industry, Singapore. Economic Survey of Singapore.

Tan, Ronald. "Singapore's Eighth Wonder". *Business Times*, Singapore, 9 November 2009.

URBANIZATION IN SOUTHEAST ASIA: DEVELOPING SMART CITIES FOR THE FUTURE?

Moe Thuzar

Cities in Southeast Asia are now faced with the strategic choice of whether economic dynamism comes at the cost of a liveable city. Pollution, concentration of population, congestion, and poor environment all contribute to this dilemma. To prevent future generations being saddled with the legacy of poor urban planning and development failure, one option is to manage the region's urbanization processes by developing "smart cities". Smart cities of the future will need sustainable urban development policies where all residents, including the poor, can live well and the attraction of the towns and cities is preserved.

Good urban planning underpins the development of a smart city. Characteristics of a smart city have been identified as smart economy, smart people, smart governance, smart mobility, smart environment, and smart living (Giffinger 2007). Smart cities are thus cities that have a high quality of life; those that pursue sustainable economic development through investments in human and social capital, and traditional and modern communications infrastructure (transport and information commmunication technology); and manage natural resources through participatory policies. Smart cities should also be sustainable, converging economic, social, and environmental goals.

Urbanization in Southeast Asia: The Need for Smart Cities

Southeast Asia has a variety of urban manifestations: three megacities (Bangkok, Jakarta, and Manila) with populations in excess of ten million; a city state (Singapore); three countries (Brunei, Malaysia, the Philippines) with over 50 per cent of the population living in urban areas; and seven with predominantly rural populations (Cambodia, Indonesia, Lao PDR, Myanmar, Thailand, Timor-Leste, Vietnam) (Population Reference Bureau 2009).

The United Nations Population Division's *World Urbanisation Prospects 2009 Revision* estimates that 65 per cent of the population in Southeast Asia will live in urban areas by 2050, a significant increase from today's 41.8 per cent. Even in countries with large rural populations, cities are at the centre of economic growth in Southeast Asia. While there are variations throughout the region, most urban places are unable to provide adequate employment, shelter, security, infrastructure, and services to their growing urban populations.

There is growing recognition that the quality of urban development affects the prospects for development, nationally as well as at the regional level.

Although all Southeast Asian countries — particularly the members of ASEAN — strive for better standards of living with sustainable livelihoods, the different urban scenarios across the region require different prescriptions for their development goals.

Urbanization has economic, infrastructure, social, environmental, and governance dimensions. Addressing the environmental, social, and economic implications of rapid urbanization requires flexibility, responsiveness, and innovation in dealing with cross-cutting, interrelated issues.

Economically, cities are engines of growth, but they need to remain competitive in the global economy. Formal employment creation is not keeping pace with economic growth. More needs to be done to create jobs and ensure higher-skilled labour. Development of urban infrastructure and services is essential for sustained economic growth, poverty reduction, and environmental sustainability. Yet, there are intra-urban inequalities (of income, access, and power) within and between urban areas.

On the environment front, cities and towns have large ecological footprints. They are often polluters of the urban environment in pursuing economic growth to reduce poverty and expand infrastructure. Many developing countries prioritize economic growth in national development agendas, while environmental clean-up often comes as an afterthought. With 36 per cent of the urban population of Southeast Asia living in low-elevation coastal zones and many more in low-lying rural areas, the region is vulnerable to sea-level rises. Cities thus face significant environmental challenges — clean air, clean water, waste management, dealing with toxic wastes, and clean energy. Neglecting these environmental challenges can lead to loss of talented people and businesses that are vital to the development and growth of cities.

Governments are thus faced with the challenge of meeting the needs of more prosperous, better educated, more demanding, and less patient urban populations. Developing smart cities can help governments address the challenges of sustaining the level of economic growth within a constantly changing global economy; reducing urban (and rural) poverty through more inclusive policies; and protecting local environments by mitigating and adapting to climate change.

URBANIZATION IN SOUTHEAST ASIA (continued)

Liveability of Smart Cities

Smart cities have the potential to become the protectors of the environment. Smart cities should also ensure that urban environments are "liveable", attracting and retaining talented people who contribute to the vibrancy of cities. The key elements of a liveable city vary, depending on the priorities and level of development in a country. Most definitions of a liveable city try to encompass all aspects of environment, social, cultural, infrastructure, governance, and participation.

To address the necessity of creating liveable urban spaces, Southeast Asian cities are considering the concept of green urban spaces. As early as 1987, Olembo and Rham have highlighted that "the quality of urban life depends largely on the amount and quality of green space within it or close to it", noting that municipal intervention is often limited to street planning, resulting in many new Third World urban areas being commonly treeless. They observed that creation of green urban spaces seems possible only when the standard of living and education has risen significantly. Singapore is cited as having the best record, among other cities in Southeast Asia and Latin America.

In recent years, urban green spaces have evolved from landscaped parks to more naturalistic habitats that complement native wildlife and urban biodiversity. These green spaces are seen as contributing to city revitalization, stimulating real estate value and local economies, encouraging community participation, and, ultimately, increasing social cohesion. As the "lungs of the city", their planning and design need to be integrated into overall urban planning to achieve environmental sustainability (Laquian 2008).

Still, no Asian — let alone Southeast Asian — city has broken through yet to the top ten liveable cities, although Singapore ranks highest among the Asian cities (at 28th position followed by Tokyo at 40th; Mercer 2010). A new Global Liveable Cities Index commissioned by Singapore's Centre for Liveable Cities, released at the June 2010 World Cities Summit, ranks Singapore 3rd behind Geneva and Zurich in a list of 64 cities (*Straits Times*, 29 June 2010). A work in progress, the five criteria for this new index are domestic security and stability; good governance and effective leadership; economic vibrancy and competitiveness; quality of life and diversity; and environmental friendliness and sustainability (Chan 2010).

The Regional Dimension

In many developing and transition economies, including those in Southeast Asia, urbanization outpaces the authorities' administrative and urban development capacities. As cities are not just economic and political centres but also major sources of social renewal, developing smart cities in the region depends on:

- creating liveable urban environments;
- reducing urban environmental and health risks effectively;
- allowing all sectors of society to participate in the social and political aspects of urban life and benefit from economic progress;
- offering urban integration support for migrants to the cities;
- transforming cities into hubs, linking rural regions with the global economy; and
- building alliances among towns and cities to solve common problems more effectively.

Governments provide an overarching framework of governance structures, coordination of policies, and macroeconomic policies at the national level. However, the role of government extends only to ensuring and promoting the right conditions for innovation to take place. Innovation still takes place at local levels, led by the private sector. Engaging the community is also important in developing well-targeted policies.

This is well-recognized by many in the region. Southeast Asian countries are eager to learn more of, and replicate, the success factors that have encouraged smart and sustainable growth of cities as engines of development. The Sino-Singapore Tianjin Eco-City initiative is a good example of how partnerships among cities can encourage convergence in addressing economic, social, and environmental goals in a well-balanced manner.

As countries in Southeast Asia move closer to their goal of regional integration — particularly economic integration — by 2015, it is becoming clear that cities and sub-regions (or city-regions) are key to the process. The Master Plan for ASEAN Connectivity adopted by the 17th ASEAN Summit in October 2010 highlights the importance of bringing together cities and towns under a coherent strategy that will stimulate economic growth and bridge regional disparities. This strategy also includes linkages with external partners, especially those in East Asia. With regional cooperation today becoming more and more focused on trade facilitation, the changing urban landscape of Southeast Asia will see even more activity among the secondary cities and smaller towns of the region, with primary cities also continuing to grow.

URBANIZATION IN SOUTHEAST ASIA (continued)

If these important nodes — which bring about closer connections within the region and with the rest of the world — are "smart" as well, the result will be a successful region where cities and towns are linked and work together for prosperity, equity, and sustainability.

The region's planners and practitioners certainly have their work cut out for them.

References

Chan, Joanne. "S'pore Emerges as Most Liveable Asian City in New Global Liveable Cities Index", 29 June 2010 <http://www.channelnewsasia.com/stories/singaporelocalnews/view/1066468/1/.html>.

Giffinger, Rudolf et al. "Smart Cities — Ranking of European Medium-sized Cities" <http:/www.smart-cities.eu/download/smart_cities_final_report.pdf> (accessed 11 November 2010).

Laquian, A.A. "The Planning and Governance of Asia's Mega Urban Regions", 2008.

Mercer. "Top 50 Cities: Quality of Living Ranking" <http://www.mercer.com/press-releases/quality-of-living-report-2010#City_Ranking_Tables>.

Olembo, R.J. and P.D. Rham. "In Two Different Worlds". *Unasylva*, no. 155 (1987) <http://www.fao.org/docrep/s1930E/s1930e00.HTM>.

Population Reference Bureau. *2009 World Population Data Sheet*. Washington, DC: Population Reference Bureau, 2009.

APEC: LOOKING BACK AND LOOKING FORWARD
Hikari Ishido

APEC 2010–11 and Its Longer-term Implications

The Asia Pacific region is where the diversity of economic operations (or even "civilizations") meet: the free trade tenet coexists (if not collides) with an economic "cooperationism". APEC (Asia Pacific Economic-Cooperation) is the premier forum in this region for addressing economic cooperation, currently in the field of trade and investment liberalization and facilitation (TILF), as symbolized in its ambitious Bogor Goals.

APEC 2010 was the occasion for APEC to evaluate these all-important Bogor Goals for thirteen APEC member economies. A new set of post-Bogor priorities will be strategically devised in 2011 with a view to realizing the "new growth strategy" outlined in APEC's "Press Statement: United States-Japan Cooperation on APEC" (29 March 2010). As heralded in the statement, the concept of "balanced, inclusive, environmentally sustainable, and knowledge-based" economic growth was newly introduced as APEC's near-future focal agendas in the "The Yokohama Vision — Bogor and Beyond", released by the leaders of APEC member economies on 14 November 2010, together with the traditional TILF agenda. The period 2010–11 is therefore expected to set a longer-term direction in that APEC's fundamental policy stance, or "philosophy", is to be addressed in "practical and concrete" terms.

Static and Dynamic Impacts of an APEC-wide Economic Integration

A total of thirteen members of APEC underwent the evaluation of the Bogor Goals in 2010. The thirteen economies were as follows: Australia, Canada, Chile, Hong Kong China, Japan, Korea, Malaysia, Mexico, New Zealand, Peru, Singapore, Chinese Taipei, and the United States. It seems that five of these economies (Australia, Canada, Japan, New Zealand, and the United States) are considered as developed, the remaining eight economies had made a strategic decision to benefit from TILF, thus voluntarily applying to be evaluated on their achievement of the Bogor Goals. The Yokohama Vision has declared that that "while more work remains to be done, these 13 economies have made significant progress toward achieving the Bogor Goals".

Table 1 provides import tariffs (both bound and applied) of the APEC members based on the most recent year of reporting available. Tariffs have been reduced according to the World Trade Organization (WTO)'s schedule and

Table 1. Import Tariffs of the APEC Members

Economy	Simple Average Bound Tariff (%)	Simple Average Applied Tariff (%)	Year of Reporting
Australia	10.27	3.53	2006
Canada	5.0	3.7	2009
Chile	25.1	6.0	2009
Hong Kong, China	0	0	2006
Japan	6.9	6.5	2009
Korea	17.2	12.8	2006
Malaysia	14.5	7.7	2009
Mexico	36.0	10.9	2008
New Zealand	12.0	3.4	2006
Peru	30.1	5.0	2008
Singapore	5.3	0	2009
Chinese Taipei	5.71	5.67	2006
United States	4.8	4.8	2006
Simple average of the above thirteen economies	13.9	5.4	Various
Simple average of the above thirteen economies in 2000 (as a reference)	14.5	7.2	2000
Brunei	27.8	3.6	2008
China	10.0	9.9	2006
Indonesia	37.24	7.64	2009
Papua New Guinea	n.a.	n.a.	
Philippines	25.44	6.23	2008
Russia	n.a.	11.9	2005
Thailand	28.97	12.43	2009
Vietnam	n.a.	11.79	2008

NOTES: The top thirteen economies underwent the evaluation of the Bogor Goals in 2010.
SOURCE: Most recent Individual Action Plans (IAP) for the section "Tariffs" at <http://www.apec-iap.org/>.

the level of tariffs listed in the table range between zero and 12.8 (on the applied basis) and between zero and 37.24 (on the bound basis). As for the twelve economies undergoing evaluation of the Bogor Goals, the simple averages of their bound tariff and applied tariff stand at 13.9 and 5.4 respectively. Considering the separate calculation done for the twelve economies (14.5 and 7.2 respectively for 2000), there has been a reduction.

In the context of the discussion of economic integration, a "static" impact signifies the immediate consequence of the tariff reduction, i.e., cheap importation of foreign commodities. Judging from Table 1, there indeed is a "static" impact expected out of APEC member economies' further tariff reduction (either on the applied or bound basis).

What should be noted here is that only a static impact (i.e., tariff reduction) is considered when observing tariff information. Put differently, consideration to tariff alone neglects the *dynamic* aspects of an open regionalism, either through investment attraction, or service-sector liberalization. In theoretical terms, capital accumulation and/or productivity enhancement can result from economic integration (Baldwin 2004; Baldwin et al. 2003). In the overall context of APEC, what is called economic and technical cooperation (ECOTECH), as discussed below, is the actual channel through which to achieve dynamic capital accumulation and productivity enhancement. Indeed, the APEC process chaired by Japan in 2010 has the theme "Change and Action", which, theoretically speaking, connotes those dynamic economic impacts.

The Scenario of an APEC-wide Economic Integration

From the 1990s onwards, the region has been witnessing the spread of regional economic integration (REI) endeavours.[1] The "density" of such trade agreements stands at 0.30 (i.e., 62 REI agreements divided by 210 possible combinations, according to the author's calculations). What could be an outcome of this proliferation of regional trade agreements or free trade agreements (RTAs/FTAs)? As is well known, the economic impacts of formulating RTAs/FTAs range from trade creation (a static impact) to capital accumulation as well as productivity enhancement (dynamic impacts). Importantly, these features of RTAs/FTAs arise from the artificially created "exclusivity". Then the "race to be the first",[2] or so-called domino effect, might result among those trading blocs. What should be noted here is the possibility of a renewed commitment toward going back to the WTO-based multilateralism. Figure 1 suggested by Petri (2008) depicts the possibility that as mutually exclusive RTAs/FTAs proliferate in number, the "density" of economies covered by certain RTAs/FTAs increases, hence the intended benefits of exclusivity gradually decrease, as indicated by the downward sloping curve in the Figure.

On the other hand, the costs of complexity, arising from the very coexistence of variously administered RTAs/FTAs, increase (this is the so-called "spaghetti bowl" effect), thereby making the upward sloping curve in the figure. At the intersection between the benefits curve and costs curve, which will inevitably be attained as the number of RTAs/FTAs increase over time, the so-far self-reinforcing spread of bilateral as well as plurilateral trade agreements loses momentum, thus paving the way back to the WTO-based multilateralism.

Currently, the all important policy direction concerns the proposed Free Trade Area of the Asia Pacific (FTAAP). And an important and concrete vehicle toward a full-fledged FTAAP is the Trans Pacific Strategic Economic Partnership Agreement (TPP), which is already in effect separately from the APEC process, by Brunei, Chile, New Zealand, and

APEC: LOOKING BACK AND LOOKING FORWARDS (continued)

Figure 1. Density and Benefits/Costs of RTAs/FTAs

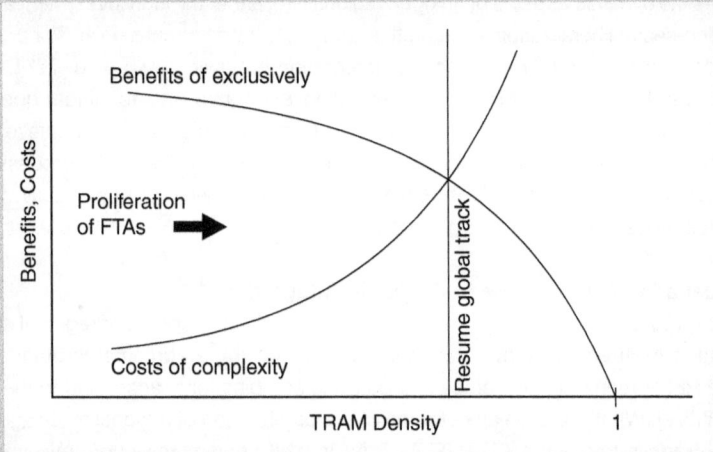

Benefits of exclusively

Benefits, Costs

Proliferation
of FTAs ➡

Resume global track

Costs of complexity

TRAM Density   1

Source: Petri (2008).

Singapore. Other economies, including the United States, Australia, Peru, Vietnam, and Japan, have shown their interest in joining TPP. Making TPP a promising avenue toward an FTAAP would facilitate benefiting from tangible ECOTECH projects in the four fields noted above, since diplomatic/policy resources could be focused more on the substance of REI, including ECOTECH at APEC.

The Way Forward: Restoring the Original APEC Feature of "Cooperationism"

APEC should sustain the original APEC feature of "cooperation" and formulate and implement concrete projects. Indeed, dynamic impacts arising from APEC's new cooperation-oriented agenda (as discussed in the previous section) are seen to be more promising than the static conduct of just eliminating the already low tariff rates in order to enjoy marginally cheaper imported products, although measuring such dynamic potential beforehand remains out of reach. In order to ensure such dynamic gains — as emphasized by Schumpeter (1926) — the

Asia Pacific region's multi-layered existence of RTAs/FTAs should be streamlined with a view to enable new combinations, especially of productive resources and markets in the Asia Pacific region. "Change and Action", the main theme of APEC 2010, should actually function as the dynamic and practical driving force through which to further boost an Asia Pacific–wide economic cooperation. It is expected that APEC, as the world's most geographically comprehensive forum, will prove to be the main vehicle in the Asia Pacific region's cooperation-based community building effort.

Notes

1. REI is treated as one of the main pillars of the APEC 2010.
2. As Baldwin (2004) suggests, the first signatory to particular RTAs/FTAs will enjoy the "exclusivity" thereof, revealed as higher profit margins as well as larger profits of the commodities traded than those captured by latecomer signatories.

References

Baldwin, Richard. *The Spoke Trap: Hub and Spoke Bilateralism in East Asia*. CNAEC Research Series 04-02, Korea Institute for International Economic Policy, 2004.

Baldwin, Richard, Rikard Foreslid, Philippe Martin, Gianmarco Ottaviano, and Frederic Robert-Nocoud, *Economic Geography and Public Policy*. New Jersey: Princeton University Press, 2003.

Petri, Peter A. "Multitrack Integration in East Asian Trade: Noodle Bowl or Matrix?" *Asia Pacific Issues*, no. 86 (2008).

Schumpeter, Joseph. *Theorie Der Wirtschaftlichen Entwicklung* (transl 1934, *The Theory of Economic Development: An Inquiry into Profits, Capital, Credit, Interest and the Business Cycle*).

NEW ECONOMIC MODEL:
WHAT LIES AHEAD FOR MALAYSIA

Kian-Teng Kwek

The road ahead for Malaysia to become a high-income nation is indeed challenging. Not only has Malaysia been affected by the global imbalance between West and East through trade and capital flows, but Malaysia's middle income trap issues are structurally complex and stem from deep-seated political economy issues. As the world is increasingly globalized and connected, Malaysia has been slowing down in terms of real growth in income. Malaysia must accept this new reality, and to leapfrog to a developed nation status by 2020 it must leverage on measures to achieve greater openness to globalization.

The Prime Minister Datuk Seri Najib Razak, the sixth Prime Minister of Malaysia, is poised to lead Malaysia through a national transformation programme through the New Economic Model (NEM). As stated in an old Chinese New Year blessing, "With three-yang begins prosperity", so the NEM is framed in three goals. These three goals are (1) a high income economy (US$15,000 to US$20,000 by 2020), (2) a sustainable economy (meeting present needs without compromising future generations), and (3) an inclusive economy (enabling all communities to benefit from the wealth of the country).

The Prime Minister articulated his aspirations in the National Transformation Programme which consists of four pillars to be launched over two years. The pillars are:

1. The New Economic Model (NEM), whose goals are to be achieved through an Economic Transformation Programme (ETP) which will propel Malaysia to an advanced nation status with a high income, and an inclusive and sustainable economy. The ETP will be driven by eight Strategic Reform Initiatives (SRIs) which will form the basis of the relevant policy measures.
2. The 1Malaysia, People First, Performance Now concept to unite all Malaysians to face the challenges ahead.
3. The Government Transformation Programme (GTP) to strengthen public services in the National Key Result Areas (NKRAs).
4. The 10th Malaysia Plan 2011–2015 and the 11th Malaysia Plan 2016–2020.

The ETP has two parts: the SRIs of the NEM and the National Key Economic Areas (NKEAs). The PEMANDU (Performance Management and Delivery Unit), headed by Datuk Seri Idris Jala, is tasked with managing the ETP and working on the implementation aspects of the NKEAS and identified Entry Point Projects (EPP). The NEM Part 1 was launched on 30 March 2010 and the NEM Concluding Part was launched on 3 November 2010.

The measures underlying the SRIs are critical to the success of the NKEAs. They are:

1. Re-energizing the private sector
2. Developing a quality workforce and reducing dependency on foreign labour
3. Creating a competitive domestic economy
4. Strengthening of the public sector
5. Transparent and market-friendly affirmative action
6. Building the knowledge-base infrastructure
7. Enhancing the sources of growth
8. Ensuring sustainability of growth

The NEM has stimulated much debate since its launch in March. The main debate was on Malaysia's New Economic Policy (NEP) which was first announced in 1970 as the principal policy response to the post-election race riots of 13 May. The debate centred on furthering the need for inclusivity. Malaysia has succeeded in building a bumiputera professional community, but it has not yet succeeded in creating a globally competitive bumiputera entrepreneurial community, which can only emerge when greater competition comes into play. The NEP was an ambitious socio-economic restructuring affirmative action programme launched by the Malaysian Government in 1971 under the second Prime Minister Tun Abdul Razak, the father of the current Prime Minister Najib.

Clearly, the NEM aims to raise the incomes of the poor, who constitute 40 per cent of Malaysian households that are still earning less than RM1,500 a month. The NEM aims to address this income disparity. Measures are needed now to narrow the economic differences prevalent in Sabah and Sarawak as well as in the rural areas of the Peninsula. In contrast, the NEP aimed at achieving a 30 per cent share of the economy for the bumiputra, while reducing poverty.

Sadly, many studies have shown that there is a huge gap between the incomes of the Malaysian rich and those 40 per cent of the Malaysian poor. The government has realized that Malaysia has reached a critical point in its economic development. If growth continues to slow, it will translate to having less resources for distribution. Malaysia, under the current speed of globalization also faces a brain drain where people and scarce capital have left to join other supply chains. Thus, Malaysia's true danger is slipping further down the middle-income trap.

The real debate is on how fast Malaysia can revive growth and continue to have resources to expand inclusivity. Efficiency is again the key to success for Malaysia to become a high income nation. The government forecast in October

NEW ECONOMIC MODEL: WHAT LIES AHEAD FOR MALAYSIA (continued)

2009 that GDP would expand by 2 to 3 per cent in 2010 after shrinking 3 per cent in 2009. However, with a good upward forecast revision, growth has expanded to 6 per cent for 2010. The real GDP growth rate in Q2 2010 was 8.9 per cent and 5.3 per cent in Q3 2010 respectively. The actual real GDP increased from RM138,520 million to RM141,895 million from Q2 to Q3. With such robust growth, the economy is believed to be on the right track.

Other key signals in the market are Malaysia's Central Bank raising its benchmark interest rate for the first time in almost four years, saying that the economy's recovery is "firmly established" as the nation emerges from its first recession in a decade. Exports grew at twice the pace the government had predicted earlier as the global recovery revived shipments of goods such as palm oil and computer chips.

However, the ETP requires that by 2020 Malaysian gross national income (GNI) be in the range of US$475–525 billion with a growth rate of 6 to 7 per cent. A simulation reveals that to reach the desired GNI of US$525 billion by 2020, a real growth rate of 9 to 9.5 per cent is required. A 6.5 to 7 per cent real growth rate may bring us there, but should there be a great hike in the price of oil to US$200, or even a catastrophic natural disaster (unlike the global financial crisis of 2008), any decent growth rate would be diverted from its norm or the long-run trajectory growth path.

The next question is whether Malaysia can achieve high income status by mega spending on infrastructure. An alternative to this economic transformation or leapfrogging is the re-energizing of the private sector to narrow income disparities and increase investment in training and upgrading human capital.

However, there has been some difficulty in attracting foreign investors. One reason for this may be that both local and foreign investors feel that the Government-Linked Companies (GLIC) like Khazanah, MKD, EPF, and PNB have been venturing beyond their given mandates. Indirectly, these giant GLICs are viewed as competing directly with private businesses and hence crowding out private investments.

Mutually, business opportunities for the private sector are limited locally, and thus it has become more profitable to invest abroad. More specifically, there is a conflict of objectives among these 445 GLICs, i.e., the difficulty of delivering social objectives but operating for profit.

The Malaysian Government knows that the current structure cannot be changed overnight, but small steps are necessary to start these reforms. How these steps are undertaken will be crucial for Malaysia's economic transformation in the years ahead.

THE ASEAN-10

Brunei Darussalam

Lee Poh Onn

Brunei had a recorded population of about 406,200 (2009 government estimates; EIU 2010). Per capita constant GDP based on purchasing power parity (international dollars) was 47,200 in 2010 (IMF 2010).

Brunei Darussalam's economic growth prospects in 2011 and 2012 are expected to better the real GDP growth rate in 2010. Which is expected to grow by only 0.5 per cent. Higher real growth rates of above 1 per cent are projected during the forecast period, with inflation rates (average consumer prices) contained at 1.8 per cent in both 2011 and 2012. Unemployment is also not expected to exceed four per cent during the forecast period.

BRUNEI DARUSSALAM

- Pick-up in the global economy in 2010, with the recovery in the U.S., Japanese, EU, and ASEAN economies will have positive spillovers for Brunei Darussalam in 2011 and 2012.

- Despite falls in the current account and fiscal surpluses in 2008 and 2009 due to the global financial and economic crisis, the Bruneian economy has remained stable with its banking system intact.

- Real GDP for 2011 and 2012 is expected to be in positive territory.

- The strength of Brunei's recovery is however dependent on the extent of the global economic recovery as well as the attendant prices of oil and gas in 2011 and 2012.

Current account surpluses and fiscal surpluses, while positive, have fallen in 2008 and 2009, but are set to improve from 2010 onwards with higher oil and gas prices and a recovery in foreign asset prices. The current account balance is expected to be about US$5.183 billion in 2010, and US$5.438 billion and US$5.726 billion in 2011 and 2012 respectively.

Growth Forecast for 2011 and 2012

During the forecast period of 2011 and 2012, real GDP is expected to increase by 1.01 and 1.22 respectively (IMF 2010). Growth rates will be in the positive territory during the forecast period because of the earnings from the oil and gas sector, continuing development of Brunei's ecotourism industry, exports from the completed methanol plant project, and the continuing development of the Sungai Liang Industrial Park (SPark) project.

SPark, located on a 271-hectare site at Sungei Liang, is being developed as a world-class petrochemical hub. Besides the Muara Island Project (PMB), SPark is one of the Brunei Economic Development Board (BEDB)'s key initiatives in accelerating the nation's economic growth and expanding the employment opportunities for its people.

However, future spin-offs from SPark can only materialize if there is further participation from overseas investors. In this sense, only time will tell whether the endeavour will be an important milestone in Brunei's process of economic development and diversification.

The present US$450 million methanol plant by the Brunei Methanol Company (BMC) in SPark — a joint venture between Petroleum Brunei and two Japanese companies, Mitsubishi Gas Chemical and Itochu — was completed and has started operations in 2010. The construction of the Single Point Mooring System required to transport methanol direct to offshore tankers was also completed in 2009. Presently, Brunei is the third-largest exporter of methanol in the region, after Malaysia and Indonesia.

Brunei Darussalam: Selected Economic Indicators, 2008–2012F

	2008	2009	2010E	2011E	2012E
GDP, constant prices (B$ billion)	11.754	11.696	11.754	11.873	12.018
GDP, constant prices (% change)	-1.939	-0.493	0.499	1.012	1.22
GDP, current prices (B$ billion)	20.398	15.135	16.495	17.269	18.149
GDP, constant prices (US$ billion)	14.417	10.405	11.963	12.593	13.019
GDP per capita, constant prices (B$)	29,532.41	28,534.72	27,845.55	27,311.80	26,843.39
GDP per capita, current prices (B$)	51,251.01	36,924.31	39,075.13	39,722.34	40,535.75
GDP per capita, current prices (US$)	36,223.35	25,386.00	28,340.04	28,966.58	29,077.66
Inflation, average consumer prices (index)	108.445	110.397	112.384	114.407	116.467
Inflation, average consumer prices (% change)	2.724	1.8	1.8	1.8	1.8
Unemployment rate (% of total labour force)	3.748	3.748	3.748	3.748	3.748
Population (million)	0.398	0.41	0.422	04.35	0.448
General government revenue (B$ billion)	12.209	6.585	8.827	9.233	9.953
General government revenue (as % of GDP)	63.983	42.55	52.895	52.794	54.34
General government total expenditure (B$ billion)	6.146	6.022	6.722	6.627	6.856
General government total expenditure (as % of GDP)	32.208	38.918	40.278	37.894	37.434
Current account balance (US$ billion)	8.523	4.857	5.183	5.438	5.726
Current account balance (as % of GDP)	59.118	46.678	43.321	43.187	43.985

Note: E refers to estimates.
Source: International Monetary Fund, *World Economic Outlook Database*, October 2010.

Firm, if not higher, petroleum prices are expected to prevail in 2011 and 2012, which will help to shore up Brunei's growth over the next few years even if Brunei does not increase its petroleum production in line with demand. The oil and gas sector comprised about 70.1 per cent of Brunei's GDP in 2008 (EIU 2010). This sector's contribution to GDP is likely to remain around the same in the years to come.

The pick up of major global economies over the year explains why energy prices have been favourably high in 2010; energy prices are expected to remain around or marginally lower than the 2010 price-level bandwidth next year, as global growth is forecast to be less robust in 2011 and 2012. However, a worrisome aspect is the weakening U.S. dollar, as Bruneian oil and gas exports are priced in U.S. dollars and this may reduce the country's export revenue earnings.

Brunei's major export markets (EIU 2010) include Japan (46.1 per cent), South Korea (11.6 per cent), Indonesia (10.8 per cent), and Australia (12.1 per cent) and it imports mainly from ASEAN (51.8 per cent), United States (13 per cent), the European Union (10.3 per cent), and Japan (8.9 per cent). To the extent that the growth prospects of these countries will remain positive during the forecast period, so will Brunei's economy be influenced to move in tandem with developments in these economies.

REFERENCES

Economist Intelligence Unit (EIU). *Country Report Brunei*, September 2010.
International Monetary Fund (IMF). *World Economic Outlook Database: October 2010 Edition* < http://www.imf.org/ > (accessed 1 November 2010).

Cambodia

Jayant Menon

Cambodia's GDP contracted by 2 per cent in 2009, marking the end of a spectacular decade of economic growth. The global financial crisis led to a decline in construction, tourism, and garments exports, which accounted for the bulk of Cambodia's GDP. Apart from the

CAMBODIA

- Cambodia's economy is recovering strongly, with growth forecast to rebound to between 4 to 5 per cent in 2010 on the back of buoyant exports and tourism.

- Both the current account deficit and inflation are expected to rise as the economy recovers, and this needs to be monitored.

- The depreciating dollar could provide a boost to clothing exports and help keep the trade deficit in check, but is unlikely to make a big impact on de-dollarization in and of itself.

- Diversification of the economy is desirable, but should be pursued by initially encouraging intra- rather than inter-sectoral specialization.

reduction in export demand as a result of the slowdown in global growth, the lifting of restrictions on Chinese garment exports to the United States and the European Union at the end of 2008 compounded the negative impact on Cambodia's garment exports (Menon 2009).

Since the beginning of 2010, however, the economy has started to show signs of recovery, aided by buoyant exports and tourism receipts, and sustained growth in agricultural production. Growth is expected to return to positive territory in 2010, with the Asian Development Bank (ADB), International Monetary Fund (IMF), and World Bank expecting it to come in at around 5 per cent, but the Economist Intelligence Unit (EIU) being more pessimistic with a forecast of 4.1 per cent. Garment exports are expected to grow by 14 per cent for 2010 as a whole, while tourism is projected to pick up by 9 per cent (World Bank 2010a). Although agriculture could be affected by the late arrival of rains in some parts of the country, a new rice production and export policy should raise the exports of milled rice and shore up the agricultural sector as a whole. In 2011, GDP is forecast to pick up further to between 6–7 per cent.

Falling revenue as a result of a weak economy, accompanied by a boost in counter-cyclical government spending, increased the fiscal deficit to 6.3 per cent in 2009. Although the government has begun consolidating counter-cyclical spending, forecasts from the EIU see the deficit remaining relatively unchanged, with only a slight decrease to 5.9 per cent in 2010 and then 5.4 per cent in 2011. The IMF reported a rebound in tax revenue, with both direct and indirect cumulative tax collection through the first seven months increasing by 8 and 18 per cent respectively (IMF, 2010). However, the overall deficit continues to be financed by concessional loans and grants. Cambodia's donors have pledged about US$1.1 billion in assistance in 2010 and US$958 million in 2011, a slight increase from US$951.5 million in 2009 (EIU 2010).

Broad money (M2) growth picked up from around 5 per cent in 2008 to 35.6 per cent in 2009, as a result of efforts to boost domestic demand through monetary expansion. The onset of the global financial crisis induced the National Bank of Cambodia (NBC) to lower the reserve requirement for commercial banks to 12 per cent, but this is expected to be reversed as the economy recovers. The EIU forecasts broad money growth to slow to 28.5 per cent in 2010, and further to 25.5 per cent in 2011.

Inflation eased significantly and turned negative in 2009 (–0.7 per cent), but with the pick up in growth, inflation is forecast to reach 4 per cent in 2010, and be in the 5 per cent range in 2011. The EIU reported that local retailers have increased prices for petrol, diesel, and other fuel products in response to higher global oil prices (EIU 2010).

The current account deficit narrowed to around 5 per cent of GDP in 2009 as a result of lower oil prices and a reduced trade deficit, but is expected to widen again to 7.3 per cent in 2010 and 9.1 per cent in 2011. A deteriorating current account deficit could put further pressure on the riel to depreciate against the dollar. If this happens, it could also lead to inflationary pressures and erode the purchasing power of income earners paid in riel rather than dollars. The recent uptick in the value of the riel reflects the general depreciation of the U.S. dollar against most regional and key currencies. If the dollar continues its trend depreciation, this could boost the competitiveness of Cambodia's clothing exports (see below), and reel in the trade deficit to some degree. Gross international reserves are expected to reach $3.7 billion in 2010, up slightly from $3.3 billion at end-2009.

Effects of a Depreciating U.S. Dollar on the Cambodian Economy

The value of the U.S. dollar against most major currencies, as well as the majority of regional currencies, has been on a downward trend over the recent past. The announcement in November 2010 that the Federal Reserve would buy up Treasury debt at a rate of around US$75 billion per month to the end of June 2011, amounting to a total of $600, is likely to contribute further to the trend decline in the value of the U.S. dollar. Most of this quantitative easing will result in a further movement of short-term capital, or hot money, to this region seeking higher yields. Very little of it is likely to be spent in the United States itself. This is likely to put further upward pressure on currencies in the region.

How is this likely to affect the Cambodian economy? In particular, how is the trend of depreciation of the U.S. currency likely to affect the competitiveness of Cambodia's exports? Since the U.S. dollar is Cambodia's de facto currency, this implies that for exports, both domestic costs and international receipts are largely determined in U.S. dollars. For example, it is widely known that wages of workers in the clothing industry are set and paid in U.S. dollars. For most of its export competitors, on the other hand, it is only international receipts that are determined in U.S. dollars, while domestic costs are determined largely in their respective home currencies. For these countries, domestic costs measured in US dollars will rise, while domestic costs in Cambodia will remain unchanged. Another way of looking at this is to consider profit margins of exporters. If world prices (in U.S. dollars) remain unchanged, a depreciating dollar will squeeze the profit margins of exporters measured in their home currency, but will not have any impact on profit margins in Cambodia since dollar margins will remain unchanged. This will result in improved competitiveness of Cambodian exports that are invoiced in U.S. dollars. This effect could be particularly important for Cambodia's clothing exports.

If the trend depreciation of the dollar continues for long, then the status of the dollar as a reliable store of value is also likely to be eroded. That is, the tendency to use dollars as a store of value may diminish over time. This could result in some increase in saving in riel, especially if the riel starts appreciating in a sustained way. This will contribute to the process of de-dollarization in the longer-term. Whether this results in a substantial switch to saving in riel is unclear, at least in the short-run. It may lead to a switch to gold, as we see in Vietnam, or to another relatively accessible and appreciating currency, such as baht or yuan. In short, while a declining dollar will help in the process of de-dollarization, the availability of other options for holding savings suggests that the real solution still lies with improving overall confidence in the riel. A declining dollar alone will not be sufficient for de-dollarization.

Diversifying the Cambodian Economy

In 2008, garments accounted for 80 per cent of Cambodia's total exports, of which close to 62 per cent were exported to the United States. The fall in Cambodia's exports earnings as a result of the global financial crisis highlighted its vulnerability to external shocks. Even more worrisome is the fact that garment exports from Cambodia contracted by more than its competitors in the region (such as Bangladesh). Cambodia clearly needs to diversify and reduce its reliance on a narrow range of commodities and markets in order to reduce its vulnerability to external shocks.

In terms of commodity diversification, Cambodia could either shift resources towards new activities within sectors (intra-sectoral specialization), or shift resources across sectors (inter-sectoral specialization). Inter-sectoral diversification would involve changes to the shares of GDP accounted for by the key sectors — agriculture, manufacturing, and services — while intra-sectoral diversification could leave these shares relatively unchanged. There are a number of reasons why intra-sectoral specialization is to be preferred if pursuing a policy of diversification. The adjustment cost associated with intra-regional specialization is likely to be much lower than inter-sectoral specialization. This is because intra-sectoral specialization does not require inter-sectoral factor movements. It is likely that factors of production can be moved more easily across activities within a sector, with greater similarity in factor intensities, than they can across sectors, where factor intensities are likely to vary more widely. Trade expansion through inter-sectoral specialization is more likely to require factor transfer from export-oriented industries to import-competing industries, whereas trade expansion through intra-sectoral specialization may only require factor transfer within export-oriented industries (Menon and Melendez 2010).

A number of recent studies provide a number of options for diversifying Cambodia's exports through intra-sectoral specialization (ADB 2010a; Economic Institute of Cambodia 2007; World Bank 2009). Within the garments sector, there remains considerable room for improving productivity and increasing value added. The EIC cites data from the customs department which revealed that 95 per cent of Cambodia's garment exports are in the knitted or crocheted category, most of which are concentrated in a few product categories (sweaters, pullovers, vests, women's or girl's suits, ensembles, and men's or boy's suits. Moreover, the Cambodian garment industry mainly focuses on basic construction and design, with very little added value. With the proper investment strategy, improvements in productivity could allow Cambodian factories to improve quality and produce higher-priced garments with more design and labour content, subsequently restoring Cambodia's competitiveness in this sector.

In a similar fashion, intra-sectoral specialization could help scale up and increase the value added of other export products where Cambodia already has a revealed comparative advantage. There is, for instance, a potential for intra-sectoral specialization in labour-intensive footwear, which accounted for 7 per cent of Cambodia's exports in 2008. Cambodia could also scale up its exports of primary unprocessed products such as rubber, non-coniferous wood, tobacco, fish and seafood, and fruits and vegetables, and subsequently embark on value-added ventures such as processing and marketing. Developing this cluster of products is critical, given that 59 per cent of the population relies on agriculture for livelihood. There is also growing evidence that the most dynamic agricultural commodities (e.g., silk, beverages, cereal preparation, preserved food, sugar preparation, manufactured tobacco, chocolate, fish, and seafood), have outperformed most manufactured goods in terms of export volumes and values (Samen 2010).

There are indications that intra-sectoral specialization is already taking place in Cambodia's rice exports at least. Cambodia's rice producers are moving up from exporting raw paddy, mostly to Vietnamese and Thai middlemen, to exporting milled rice directly to Western and Eastern Europe (Trade SWAp, 2009). The new rice production and export policy should help raise the exports of milled rice even further.

Apart from diversifying the export product base, there is also a need to diversify export markets, so that there is less reliance on demands from a small number of countries. Cambodia's garment manufacturers are already taking steps to expand their exports to the EU market (Trade SWAp, 2009).

REFERENCES

Asian Development Bank (ADB). Report and Recommendation of the President to the Board of Directors: Proposed Kingdom of Cambodia: Promoting Economic Diversification Program, Subprogram 2 (RRP CAM 38421-02). Manila: ADB, 2010a.

———. Asian Regional Integration Center (ARIC) Integration Indicators Database < http://www.aric.adb.org/indicator.php >. Manila: ADB, 2010b.

Economic Institute of Cambodia (EIC). "Export Diversification and Value Addition for Human Development", June 2007.

Economist Intelligence Unit (EIU). *Cambodia Country Report*, October 2010.

International Monetary Fund (IMF). "IMF Team Completes the 2010 Article IV Consultation Discussions with Cambodia". Press Release No. 10/334, 10 September 2010.

Menon, Jayant. "Cambodia's Persistent Dollarization: Causes and Policy Options", *ASEAN Economic Bulletin* 25, no. 2 (2008): 228–37.

———. "The Global Financial Crisis: Regional and Local Impacts". In *Annual Development Review 2008–09*. Phnom Penh: Cambodia Development Resource Institute, 2009.

Menon, Jayant and Anna Melendez. "Trade and Investment in the GMS: Remaining Challenges and the Unfinished Policy Agenda". ADB Working Paper Series in Regional Economic Integration, Manila: ADB, 2011.

Samen, Salomon. "A Primer on Export Diversification: Key Concepts, Theoretical Underpinnings and Empirical Evidence. Mimeographed. 2010.

Trade SWAp. "Top 10 Facts You Need to Know about Cambodia's Trade SWAp: An Interview of H.E. PAN Sorasak, Secretary of State, Ministry of Commerce". *Trade SWAp* 1, no. 1 (2009): 2–3.

Cambodia: Selected Economic Indicators, 2004–2012F

	2005	2006	2007	2008	2009E	2010F	2011F	2012F
GDP growth (% change)								
IMF World Economic Outlook, October 2010	13.25	10.771	10.213	6.692	-1.957	4.766	6.816	6.472
WB Global Economic Prospects, Summer 2010	13.3	10.8	10.2	6.7	-2	4.8	6	6.5
ADB Asian Development Outlook 2010, Update	13.3	10.8	10.2	6.7	-2	5	6	
Economist Intelligence Unit, Cambodia Country Report, October 2010	13.3	10.8	10.2	5.0b	-1.5	4.1	5.1	
— Agriculture sector growth (% change)	15.7	5.5	5	2.0b	3	4	4.5	
— Industry sector growth (% change)	12.7	18.3	8.4	8.0b	-6.5	4.5	6	
— Services sector growth (% change)	13.1	10.1	10.1	4.9b	-0.9	3.9	4.9	
Exports, goods fob (US$ million)	2,910	3,692	4,089	4,708	4,302*	5,154	5,543	
Imports, goods fob (US$ million)	-3,918	-4,771	-5,439	-6,509	-5,876*	-6,724	-7,331	
Trade balance (US$ million)	-1,008	-1,079	-1,351	-1,800	-1,574*	-1,570	-1,788	
Current account balance (% of GDP)								
IMF World Economic Outlook, October 2010	-3.824	-0.645	-2.454	-6.209	-5.173	-7.292	-9.117	-9.627
Inflation/CPI average (% change)								
IMF World Economic Outlook, October 2010	6.349	6.143	7.668	24.997	-0.663	3.972	5.155	3.697
ADB Asian Development Outlook 2010, Update	6.4	6.1	7.7	25	0.8	4	5	
M2 money supply growth (% change)	15.8	40.5	61.8	5.4	35.6*	28.5	25.5	
Fiscal balance (as % of GDP)	-2.5	-2.7	-2.9	-2.9b	-6.3	-5.9	-5.4	

Cambodia: Selected Economic Indicators, 2004–2012F *(continued)*

	2005	2006	2007	2008	2009E	2010F	2011F	2012F
Total debt outstanding and disbursed (US$ million), ADB Statistical Database System	3,515	3,527	3,761	4,127	..	..	..	..
Long term debt (US$ million), ADB Statistical Database System	3,154.747	3,317.688	3,537.077	3,892.063	..	..	..	..
Debt service ratio (as % of XGS), ADB Statistical Database System	0.72936	0.5815	0.51023	0.63294	..	..	..	..
Foreign exchange reserves (US$ million)	1,159	1,411	2,143	2,641	3,288*	3,740	4,001	
Exchange rate at year-end (S$/US$1)	4,112	4,057	3,999	4,077	4,165*	4,242	4,276	

NOTES: E refers to estimates; F refers to forecasts; * actual.
SOURCES: Unless otherwise noted, all data are from the Economist Intelligence Unit, *Cambodia Country Report*, October 2010.

World Bank. *Cambodia Country Economic Memorandum*. Washington, DC: World Bank, 2009.

———. *World Bank October 2010 East Asia and Pacific Economic Update*. Washington, DC: World Bank, (2010a).

———. *World Bank Economic Prospects, Summer 2010*. Washington, DC: World Bank, (2010b).

Indonesia

Reza Siregar

Economic recovery is expected to be on track in 2010, with a buoyant medium-term outlook.

In July 2010, the Credit Rating Agency in Japan, Indonesia's top long-term foreign investor, upgraded Indonesian Government debt to investment grade, citing solid economic growth, political stability, and

INDONESIA

- Economic recovery is on track in 2010, with a buoyant medium-term outlook.

- Uncertainty in the global market however remains a looming risk in the near future. Despite the country's large domestic market, Indonesia cannot escape the adverse consequences of weaker-than-expected performance of the G-3 economies (the United States, Japan, and Europe).

- Volatile capital flow presents a huge challenge for the next one or two years. The transmission of abundant global liquidity and the accompanying surge in capital flows affect the domestic economy through price factors, most importantly via exchange rate and asset price.

- Attracting investment is a priority for the country to achieve its 6.6 per cent average growth in 2009–14. Two major impediments are the labour law and the dismal state of the infrastructure.

- Stronger growth momentum continues in 2011 and 2012. However, achieving the target average growth rate of 6.6 per cent for the period of 2009–14 is going to be difficult.

conservative fiscal policy. Uncertainty in the global market however remains a looming risk in the near future. Despite the country's large domestic market, Indonesia cannot evade the adverse consequences of weaker-than-expected performance of the G-3 economies (the United States, Japan, and Europe) during most of 2010.

Robust private consumption continued to play a role in 2010, constituting around 60 per cent of the economy. This healthy trend was achieved despite the return of inflationary pressure. Annualized headline inflation in September 2010 was reported at around 5.8 per cent, a slight moderation from 6.4 per cent in August 2010. Nonetheless, the inflation rate during the first half of 2010 was double that of the first half of 2009. The price-of-food component was the primary driver, reporting an annualized increase of more than 13 per cent in August 2010.

Exports rose 44 per cent to $72.55 billion during the first half of 2010, while imports surged 51.99 per cent to $62.89 billion from the same period last year. That resulted in a healthy $9.63 billion trade surplus for the first half of the year, up from $8.6 billion during the same period last year. The current account balance continued to be in surplus since the third quarter of 2009, albeit moderated in 2010. The second quarter 2010 surplus was only around half of the surplus registered in the final quarter of 2009. Another notable trend is the encouraging investment growth of around 10 per cent year-on-year in the first-half of 2010, compared to around 3 per cent in 2009.

The relative vigour of the Indonesian economy and relatively high yield attracted strong surges of capital inflow in most of 2010. Most of the inflows have been in the form of portfolio capital, contributing to more than a 38 per cent hike in the Jakarta stock exchange index between May and October 2010. The strong capital inflows and the current account surplus generated strong appreciation of the rupiah. Despite active intervention by Bank Indonesia to manage the appreciation, the rupiah recorded around 5 per cent appreciation against the U.S. dollar during the first ten months of 2010. The strength of balance of payment position contributed also to a steep reserve accumulation. By the end of September 2010, the foreign exchange reserve was reported at around $84 billion, compared to around $66 billion at the end of 2009.

Living with Surging Capital Inflows

Volatile capital flow poses a vast challenge for Indonesia for the next one or two years. As uncertainty concerning economic recovery in developed economies is unlikely to dissipate any time soon, investors target emerging markets for higher yields on their investment capital. The transmission of abundant global liquidity and the accompanying surge in capital flows affect the domestic economy through price factors, most importantly via the exchange rate and asset prices. The challenge is even more complex when a large share of these flows is in the form of portfolio capital. The predominantly short-term capital must be converted to more stable and longer-term funds. During the first half of 2010, Indonesia received over $12 billion, more than double the amount during the same period of 2009. By the end of September 2010, the Jakarta stock exchange index was reported at around 3,500, a new peak and an increase of over 13 per cent from the previous month. This raised some concerns on the return of the asset bubble.

Consistent and credible policy measures are therefore critical in dealing with massive and volatile global liquidity. A number of policy packages have been pursued during the past one year. To curtail short-term volatility, Bank Indonesia (BI) introduced a one-month holding period for its certificate (SBI) purchased in both primary and secondary markets in June 2010. Prior to this, BI launched a concerted effort to shift the maturity structure from one-month to three- and six-month tenures and from weekly to monthly auction. Longer maturity SBIs — SBI-nine-month and SBI-twelve-month — are being considered in late 2010 with the purported aim of lengthening the maturity profile of investors.

Despite the efforts, appreciation pressures on the local currency continued to gain more momentum, especially in the last quarter of 2010. The Indonesian Handicraft and Furniture Industry Association warned that the appreciation of the Indonesian currency against the U.S. dollar is starting to have a negative impact on the industry. To make matters worse, the euro depreciated against the U.S. dollar by around 10 per cent between January and September 2010. The Eurozone has long been one of the major markets for Indonesian exports.

The significant rise of the net foreign assets of BI partly reflects the size and the frequency of open market operations that BI has done to tame the appreciation pressure on the rupiah. In turn, this raises concerns regarding the quasi-fiscal cost of this intervention activity on the balance sheet of Bank Indonesia. The cost continues to mount with the weakening of the U.S. dollar (against the rupiah) and the persistent interest-spread between the U.S. dollar yield and the rupiah yield.

Monetary policy operations in the country have also been made much more convoluted by these inflows. The external fund led to excess liquidity in the banking and corporate sector with limited spillover to the economy. Under these circumstances, market regulation and outright intervention into the banking sector must be implemented cautiously. This challenge is especially felt with the interest rate policy. Despite the effort to ease the policy rate of Bank Indonesia by 300 basis points, a similar reduction in deposit and lending rates has not occurred. To pursue reduction in deposit rates, with the expectation that such a move will also lower lending rates, BI guided fourteen banks in August 2009 to progressively bring down their deposit rates to no more than 50 basis points above the policy rate by December 2009. Banks complied with the deposit rate reduction, but lending rates have remained mostly sticky downward.

Labour and Infrastructure Impediments

Attracting investment is a priority for the country in order to achieve its 6.6 per cent average growth in 2009–14. During the past decade, investment has remained rather short of the 30 per cent level that the country achieved from 1995 to 1997. Two major impediments are the labour law and the dismal state of the infrastructure. Before 1998, public infrastructure investment stood at 5–6 per cnet of GDP. It fell dramatically in the years after the crisis, to about 1 per cent of

GDP in 2000, before picking up to 3.4 per cent of GDP in 2007. The country's "infrastructure deficit" surfaces across different sectors of the economy, including roads, electricity, and ports. Land acquisition is the primary hindrance to the progress of road construction. A revision of the 1961 law is urgently needed. The 2010 Global Competitiveness Survey of investors ranks Indonesia 96th out of the 133 countries in terms of the provision of infrastructure.

Compared with its neighbours, Indonesia also appears to be the most difficult and expensive country to hire and fire workers. The 2003 Manpower Law has deterred firms from hiring workers on a permanent basis, particularly with the severance pay estimated to be around 108 weeks' worth of salary. The high cost of hiring and firing to some extent offsets the country's relatively low wage advantage. The World Bank's *Doing Business 2010* report ranks Indonesia 149th out of 183 countries in terms of labour market flexibility.

Key Assumptions

The annualized growth rate of the economy continued to gather positive momentum for four consecutive quarters from the third quarter of 2009. The last time the economy grew at an increasing annualized quarterly rate was during 2006 and 2007. As in many parts of Asia, the sharp recovery of the export sector and investment contributed significantly to swift economic recovery in Indonesia, hence underscoring the importance of sustained global economic recovery to realize sustainable growth of the Indonesian economy.

Further quantitative easing measures announced in the last quarter of 2010 by the U.S. Federal Reserve Board System and the European Central Bank hinted at a bleak prognosis for stronger economic recovery among the developed economies in the near future. Under the present fragile global economic outlook, the Indonesian economy is forecast to grow at 6.2 per cent in 2010 and 6.5 per cent in 2011. Expecting a moderately healthier global economy, growth momentum is projected to continue in 2012, with the GDP growth rate to hit below 7 per cent.

Indonesia: Selected Economic Indicators, 2007–2012F

	2007	2008	2009	2010F	2011F	2012F
% change over previous year						
Real Gross Domestic Product	6.3	6.1	4.6	6.2	6.5	6.7
Real Private Consumption	5.0	5.3	4.9	4.9	4.9	5.0
Gross Fixed Investment	9.2	11.7	3.4	10.0	12.0	12.2
Merchandise Exports (f.o.b. US$ billion)	118.0	139.6	119.5	149.4	166.6	—
Merchandise Imports (f.o.b. US$ billion)	84.9	116.1	–84.3	–112.4	–129.7	—
Current account balance (% of GDP)	2.5	0.1	2.0	1.0	0.5	0.1
Inflation/CPI average (% change)	6.1	11.1	2.8	6.0	6.6	7.0
Fiscal balance (as % of GDP)	–1.3	–1.0	–1.6	–1.4	–1.2	–1.0
External debt (% of GDP)	32.0	33.0	28.8	26.0	24.1	22.0
Foreign exchange reserves (US$ billion)	56.9	52.1	66.1	91.5	105.0	120.0
Exchange rate at year-end (IDR/US$1)	9,419	10,950	9,403	8,900	8,600	8,100

NOTE: F refers to forecasts.
SOURCES: Consensus Forecast, International Monetary Fund Database, Asian Development Bank Database, Author's estimates.

Despite a stronger direct investment outlook, consumption continues to be the backbone of the economy for the next two to three years. Trade surplus should continue. But exports should expand only moderately, due to fragile demand from the traditional major trading partners and strong local currency. As yield and growth are expected to remain low in major world economies, strong surges of capital to Indonesia should boost inflationary pressure domestically. Price level increase is expected to reach 6 per cent in 2010, within the inflation target of Bank Indonesia. Going forward, inflationary pressure is expected to rise further with the return of stronger demand and escalating commodity prices in the global market, especially fuel and food prices.

Laos

Kyophilavong Phouphet

Economic Performance

The global financial crisis seems to have had a minor impact on the Lao economy. GDP may increase from 7.1 per cent in 2009 to 8 per cent in 2010 and 2011. A number of mining and hydropower projects have been carried out and have contributed to economic growth in the country. Economic growth in 2011 may stem from about 15 per cent growth in the industry sector, 3 per cent growth in the agricultural sector, and 6.5 per cent growth in the service sector.

Despite credit expansion during the previous year, inflation and the exchange rates have remained stable. Laos' currency, the kip, appreciated against the U.S. dollar by about 4.5 per cent in 2010. The main reasons for appreciation of the exchange rate are massive capital inflows from mining and hydropower projects, a weakened U.S. dollar, and the monetary authority's policy to stabilize the exchange rate and control inflation.

As inflation and the exchange rates are highly correlated in Laos, appreciation of the exchange rate led to lower inflation; as a result, inflation was stable at 0.1 per cent in 2009 and will increase about

---

LAOS

- Laos has recovered from the global financial crisis and has enjoyed positive rates of economic growth.

- The resource sector is still the main source of growth for the country.

- In the medium term, high growth is expected to continue due to mining and hydropower activities.

- However, the main challenge for growth is in effective macroeconomic management to deal with massive foreign capital inflows and windfall expenditures from the resource boom.

- Improving the business climate in order to increase the competitiveness of non-resource sectors is also a crucial challenge for Laos.

3 to 5 per cent in 2011. The main reasons for increased inflation are the rapid rise in food prices and credit expansion in the previous years.

Fiscal balance in Laos has improved. Laos' fiscal balance was aggravated from the impact of the global financial crisis during 2008 and 2009, but the budget deficit as a share of GDP will decrease from 6.6 per cent in 2009 to about 4.4 per cent in 2010 and 2011. The main reason for the narrowing budget deficit is increasing government revenues from mining and hydropower projects, and other tax revenues. In addition, government expenditures have increased slightly from the previous year. However, off-budget spending seemed to be considerable during 2009 and 2010.

The trade deficit has narrowed. The trade deficit decreased from US$1,017 million in 2009 to US$710 million in 2010. The main reasons for the narrowing trade deficit are expanding mineral exports and increasing electricity exports to Thailand. The external debt burden remains high, at about 50 per cent of GDP in 2010 or about 6 per cent of total exports. Most of this debt is long-term public debt and it exceeds the accepted threshold from the International Monetary Fund (IMF). However, this trend seems to have declined compared to the previous year.

Economic Outlook

Growth is expected to be robust, about 8 per cent for 2011–12.[1] This prediction assumes that the world economy will recover from the global financial crisis and that the hydropower and mining sectors will remain active. The industrial sector is forecast to continue to grow in double digits. Agriculture sector growth might decline slightly due to climate volatility, while the service sector might expand due to the expansion of private banks and the financial sector, as well as increasing tourism.

The inflation and exchange rates are expected to be stable in the medium-term. The inflation rate is expected to stabilize around 3 to 5 per cent due to increased food prices and expansion of credit from the previous year. The exchange rate (kip/US$) is expected to appreciate due to capital inflows and a weak dollar; the exchange rate will be about 8,000 in 2011–12. This figure assumes increased capital inflows from foreign direct investment, expanding mineral and electricity exports, and a prudent exchange rate policy for de-dollarization.

The trade deficit is expected to continue to narrow during 2011–12 due to increasing exports in mining and hydropower. Nam Theun 2 hydropower has exported electricity to Thailand since 2010 and it is assumed that some of the approved mining projects will begin operations and begin exporting. The ratio of budget deficit to GDP is expected to decline about 5 per cent in 2011–12 because tax revenues from the resource sector are expected to increase and the government might control expenditures.

Main Challenges to Development

There are four main challenges for the Lao economy. First, the appropriate macroeconomic adjustment to respond to massive foreign capital inflows from natural resources investment and short-to-medium term capital inflows from establishing the stock exchange market. Effective expenditure management of booming sector windfalls is also a crucial challenge for Laos. Because the recent appreciation of the real exchange rate might contract non-booming sectors by declining their competitiveness, it could hinder growth in the mid and long term. Second, the high external debt. Although Laos has made progress in reducing its external public debts, it is still at a high risk for debt distress. The stock of external debt accounted for 53 per cent of GDP at the end of 2008. Third, the improving monetary and fiscal policy discipline and banking sector reforms. The government has operated off-budget and has rising quasi-fiscal liabilities. In addition, the monetary authority has also provided loans to local government for infrastructure development. This is a risk which might lead to macroeconomic instability. Although banking reforms have improved the state-owned commercial banks' balance sheets and banking practices, the financial system is still weak and does not have financial depth. The ratio of broad money to GDP was less than 25 per cent at the end of 2008.

Fourth, the improvement of the business climate for the private sector. Despite the significant efforts of the Lao government to improve the business climate for the private sector in the previous year, the climate remains poor. Laos was ranked 167 out of 183 countries in *Doing Business 2010* published by the World Bank Group, effectively the worst rank in the region. This provides a number of warnings about

Laos: Selected Economic Indicators, 2006–2012E

	2006	2007	2008	2009	2010E	2011E	2012E
GDP growth (% change)							
Lao government	8.1	7.9	7.9	7.1	8.0	8.0	8.0
IMF	8.4	7.5	7.2	4.6	5.4	8.4	6.7
World Bank	8.1	7.5	7.0	7.0	7.8	7.7	7.7
Industry sector growth (% change)[a]	14.2	4.4	10.4	15.9	15.0	15.0	15.0
Services sector growth (% change)[a]	9.7	9.1	9.1	7.3	6.5	6.5	6.5
Agriculture sector growth (% change)[a]	2.5	8.6	3.7	3.1	3.0	3.5	3.5
Exports (US$ million)	660.0	663.0	863.0	1,500.0	1,671.0	1,935.0	2,199.0
Imports (US$ million)	1,589.0	2,156.0	2,816.0	2,517.0	2,381.0	2,977.0	3,397.0
Trade balance (US$ million)	–929.0	–1,493.0	–1,953.0	–1,017.0	–710.0	–1,042.0	–1,198.0
Current account balance (% of GDP)	–10.3	–15.8	–16.5	–13.8	–9.6	–9.6	–9.6
Inflation/CPI average (% change)[b]	4.7	5.6	3.2	0.1	3.3	3.5	3.2
M2 money supply growth (% change)[a]	37.2	58.8	18.3	31.2	28.2	28.2	28.2
Fiscal balance (as % of GDP)[b]	–3.0	–2.9	–2.0	–6.6	–4.8	–4.8	–4.8
Total debt outstanding (US$ million)	2,351.0	2,521.0	2,931.0	3,083.6	3,323.1	3,549.9	3,514.4
Long-term debt (US$ million)[c]	2,351.0	2,521.0	2,931.0	3,083.6	3,323.1	3,549.9	3,514.4
Debt service ratio (as % of exports)	3.6	4.0	4.2	6.9	6.2	6.1	5.7
Foreign exchange reserves (US$ million)	336.0	536.0	636.0	635.0	512.0	595.0	736.0
Exchange rate at year-end (S$/US$1)[a,b]	9,655.0	9,341.0	8,466.0	8,400.0	8,064.0	7,983.4	7,903.5

NOTES: E refers to estimated values.

a. Values from 2009 to 2011 are from government planning based on five-year socioeconomic development plan (2011–15) and consultation with an economist at the National Economic Research Institute (NERI).

b. This is fiscal year which starts in September.

c. Data on long-term debt is not available, assuming that total debt is long-term debt.

SOURCES: IMF (2009a and 2009b); Government of Laos (2010); World Bank (2010); Figures for 2011 and 2012 are the author's estimates.

the delays and other difficulties that private investors might expect to encounter when doing business in Laos.

NOTE

1. The Lao Government and international organizations such as the IMF, Asian Development Bank (ADB), and World Bank have predicted different rates of growth. However, the official Lao government's estimation is used here, based on the 7th Socio-Economic Development Plan (2011–2015) and in consultation with economists at the National Research Institute (NERI), Ministry of Planning and Investment.

REFERENCES

Government of Laos. *7th National Socio Economic Development Plan (NEDP) for 2011 to 2015*. Vientiane: Ministry of Planning and Investment, 2009.
International Monetary Fund. *Staff Report for the 2009 Article Consultation*. International Monetary Fund, 2009*a*.
————. *Joint IMF/World Bank Debt Sustainability Analysis 2009*. International Monetary Fund and International Development Association, 2009*b*.
World Bank. *Lao PDR: Recent Economic Development*. Vientiane: World Bank, Vientiane Office, 2010.

Malaysia

Chia Wai Mun and Li Mengling

Economic Performance

Most crisis-hit countries in Asia rebounded from the sharpest output decline since the 1930s in the second half of 2009. However, the pace of recovery is uneven and weak across geographies and sectors.

MALAYSIA

- The current account surplus is expected to remain at a high level and to underpin Malaysia's external balance fundamentals.

- Recovery in export demand will sustain modest rebound in manufacturing while services and construction will benefit from strengthening of domestic demand, especially private consumption and investment.

- The services sector will not only constitute the largest part of the economy in the coming years but will also be the most dynamic in the country.

Similarly, Malaysia pulled out from recession in the fourth quarter of 2009 with a 4.5 per cent quarterly based growth. The real GDP for the full year, however, remained contracted by 1.7 per cent. The recession is shorter and milder than expected compared to the forecast of 3 per cent decline in GDP growth.

Table 1 shows the growth rate of expenditure on GDP in three recent crises in 1998, 2001, and 2009. When compared to the 1997–98 Asian financial crisis and the 2001 dot-com bubble, the current recession is more similar to the 2001 dot-com slowdown as in both cases exports and imports fell sharply, accompanied by destocking and investment cutback. On the demand side, exports and imports dropped by 10.4 per cent and 12.3 per cent respectively. Private investment also fell by 7.5 per cent. The expansionary government spending of 3.1 per cent and marginal growth in private consumption of 0.7 per cent helped to prevent a more severe downturn. On the supply side, most of the domestic-oriented services and construction and commodity-based agricultural sector managed positive albeit slower growth. The output of these industries recovered to the pre-crisis level by the second half of 2009. However, export-oriented manufacturing was hard hit by the plunge in global demand with a contraction of 9.3 per cent in constant prices. The output of export-oriented industries in the fourth quarter of 2009 was about 7 per cent below the pre-crisis level.

Table 1. Growth Rate of Expenditure on GDP in Three Recent Crises

	1998	2001	2009
GDP	−5.3	0.5	−1.7
Imports	−18.6	−8.3	−12.3
Exports	0.5	−8.2	−10.4
Stock Changes	0.0	−2.0	−1.9
Fixed investment	−18.8	−0.5	−5.6
Government Consumption	−0.9	1.6	3.1
Private Consumption	−4.7	1.3	0.4

At a glance, the plunge in external demand hurt the exports of Malaysia with 31.3 per cent decrease from India, 26.8 per cent from the United States, 24.2 per cent from Japan, and 19.9 per cent from the European Union. International Monetary Fund (IMF) estimates show that a 1 per cent decline in U.S. and EU domestic demand could subtract an estimated 0.6 percentage points from GDP growth for Malaysia.

While the export to other markets fell by double digits, it rose by 5 per cent for China in 2009, as shown in Table 2. However, the emergence of China as Malaysia's largest export market, as shown in Figure 1, is not sufficient to fuel its export growth at double-digit level after 2010 due to the low base effect. The share of exports to other markets remained relatively unchanged except for declining U.S. share.

Since the Asian financial crisis, the average investment share of GDP between 2000 and 2007 declined about 17 per cent compared to the average share between 1990 and 1997 for Malaysia, being the most significant drop among the group of relatively more export-oriented Asian economies. Combined with the relatively stable saving pattern, the fall in investment as a share of GDP contributed to rising current account surplus in this period. The current account surplus is expected

Table 2. Export Value and Growth by Countries

	2008		2009		% Change in export value
	Value RM billion	% of total	Value RM billion	% of total	
ASEAN	170	26	141	25	−16.8
China (incl. HK)	92	14	96	17	5.0
East Asian NICs	44	7	37	7	−15.8
India	25	4	17	3	−31.3
United States	83	12	61	11	−26.8
Japan	72	11	54	10	−24.2
European Union	75	11	60	11	−19.9
Rest of World	104	16	87	16	−16.4

Figure 1. Emergence of China as Malaysia's Largest Export Market

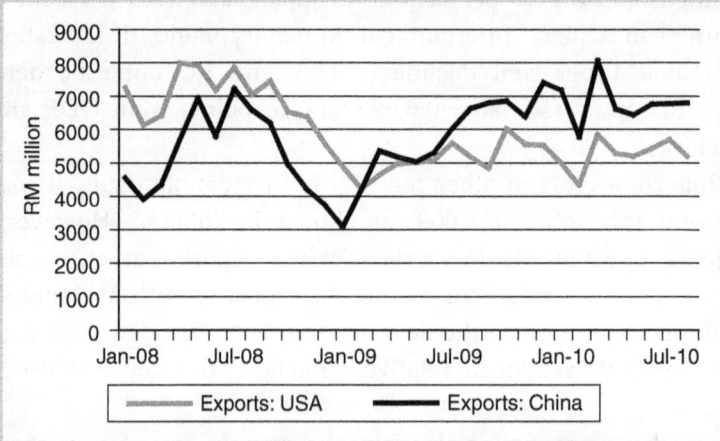

to remain at a high level and to underpin Malaysia's external balance fundamentals. The current account surplus eased from 18.1 per cent of GNP in 2008 to an estimated 16.6 per cent of GNP in 2009, while capital and financial account deficit shrank slightly from 16.5 per cent to 14.1 per cent of GNP. There is a small balance of payments surplus of RM14 billion (1.8 per cent of GNP) estimated for 2009 compared with RM19 billion (2.6 per cent of GNP) in 2008.

The currency has experienced the strongest real effective exchange rate appreciation so far in 2010, and it was close to a ten-year high in August 2010. The real effective exchange rate appreciation largely reflects higher nominal exchange rates.

Economic Outlook

With the recovery maturing in 2011, growth is expected to return to trend. 2010's economic growth is expected to reach 7 per cent and will average to 6 per cent for the years 2010–14 compared to 4 per cent in 2005–09. In 2010, economic growth is being driven by continued expansion in domestic demand due mainly to higher private consumption, a modest recovery in private investment, and sustained support from public sector spending. With the recently announced 2011 budget of RM212 billion, which is 2.8 per cent higher than the 2010 budget, growth in 2011 is expected to remain strong, supported by continued expansion in both domestic and external demand, hovering between 5 and 6 per cent.

The Malaysian economy will be fully exposed to the forces of regionalization and globalization. Asia, which already accounts for more than half of Malaysia's exports, will continue to grow in importance as a market for Malaysia. Recovery in export demand will sustain modest rebound in manufacturing while services and construction will benefit from strengthening of domestic demand, especially private consumption and investment. The services sector will not only constitute the largest part of the economy in the coming years, but will also be the most dynamic, as the government will allocate more resources into the sector to make Malaysia a high-income economy defined by an income of US$21,000 GNP per capita by 2020. Economic policies will build on Malaysia's advantages in labour, capital, natural resources, and advanced infrastructure.

The government is putting in place measures to boost infrastructure. The government will begin to implement projects outlined in the Tenth Malaysia Plan (a medium-term spending plan for 2011–15). The Mass Rapid Transit project will be implemented at the beginning of 2011 and completed by 2020. In time, improvements in infrastructure will benefit end users, enhance connectivity, and draw in additional investments.

Though global recovery is likely to remain weak and uneven, regional trade and investment flows are expected to improve further this year, supported by strong domestic demand-led growth in the BRICs, namely Brazil, Russia, India, and China. Malaysia's economy resumes modest growth this year, with the public sector reform and transformation strengthening consumer and investor confidence. It can further trigger a surge in domestic and foreign direct investment. An expanding economy from 2010, rising disposable incomes and consumer purchasing power will boost the attractiveness of the Malaysian market, although market opportunities will be constrained by the small size of the population compared with other countries in the region.

The fiscal stimulation in the global financial crisis has resulted in the fiscal deficit rising from RM36 billion (4.8 per cent of GDP) in 2008 to RM51 billion (7 per cent of GDP) in 2009 as shown in Figure 2. Likewise, total government debt has risen from 41.4 per cent of GDP to 53.3 per cent by the end of 2009. With the 2011 budget of RM212 billion, budget deficit is expected to reduce only modestly from 5.6 per cent in 2010 to 5.4 per cent in 2011. Plans to broaden the tax base have encountered strong resistance from businesses as well as consumers. The government has already watered down its new property tax and is likely to delay the introduction of a goods and services tax, originally planned for 2011. This will hamper its fiscal consolidation efforts. The government aims to move to full market pricing for a small range of goods and services by 2015.

Bank Negara Malaysia is expected to tighten monetary policy further in the second half of 2010 and in 2011 as domestic demand continues to strengthen. The Bank has begun a "normalization" cycle with a 25 basis points raise in the overnight policy rate (OPR) in March, May and July 2010, after lowering the OPR by 150 basis points from 3.5 per cent in November 2008 to 2 per cent in February 2009. We

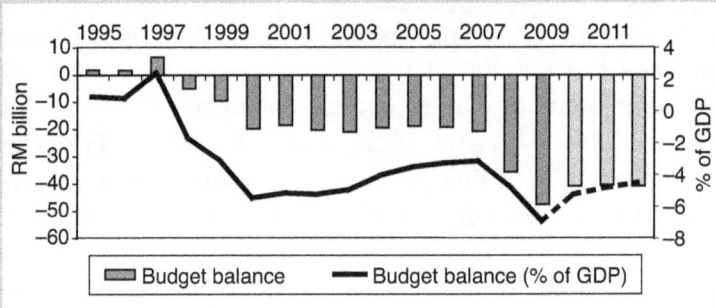

Figure 2. Trend in Budget Balance

anticipate the OPR to be kept at 2.75 per cent until the end of 2010. Over the long term, the OPR is anticipated to revert to its average long-term rate of 3.25–3.5 per cent as growth reaches the pre-crisis trend level of 5–6 per cent.

On capital flows, inflows of foreign direct investment (FDI) are expected to increase from 2010 onwards. However, owing to an intensification of competition with China, the inflows will not exceed the record of US$8.5 billion in 2007. The government will attempt to attract FDI into the country's small and medium-sized enterprise sector by offering tax incentives as well as by promoting new and existing opportunities. Compared to China, Malaysia has the advantages of a fairly well-educated workforce with relatively strong foreign-language skills and good infrastructure. This will make Malaysia remain one of the most attractive investment destinations in Southeast Asia.

The current account surplus is expected to shrink as a proportion of GDP. The surplus will fall from an estimated 17.7 per cent of GDP in 2009 to 13.5 per cent in 2012. The trade balance will make the largest contribution to the current account surplus in the short run as exports continue to exceed imports by a large margin. The services account will register a surplus. The income account has traditionally posted a deficit and it is expected to remain in the red.

The currency is expected to appreciate gradually with the better growth performance, high current account surplus and international reserves along with positive interest rate differentials and low inflation. The ringgit is expected to strengthen to RM3.25/US$ by end of 2010 and RM3.22/US$ in 2011 as Malaysia remains on a faster economic growth trajectory than the United States. The current exchange rate regime, a float managed against a trade-weighted basket of currencies, is expected to be maintained. The nominal and real effective exchange rate is projected to rise by 3–5 per cent in 2010 within the long-term average band in reflection of international price competitiveness. Further bilateral trade agreements and progress towards regional economic integration will prompt the monetary authorities to allow offshore trading in the ringgit.

Both producer and consumer prices were mostly subdued in 2009 due to disinflation rather than deflation as shown in Figure 3. The core consumer price index (CPI) remained relatively stable while imported inflation is not likely to be strong this year due to weak global demand, strong ringgit, and lower trade tariff rates. The CPI inflation is estimated to be 1.8 per cent in 2010 and 2.7 per cent in 2011, reflecting the improving economic conditions. Domestic factors account for a lower share of inflation fluctuations as Malaysia is relatively more open and exposed to global inflationary shocks. The likely introduction of a goods and services tax will result in a modest increase in overall consumer prices. The strength of the ringgit will help to contain inflationary pressures as the currency is forecast to appreciate against the U.S. dollar from 2010. The removal of trade barriers and greater regional economic integration will also help to maintain a low-inflation environment.

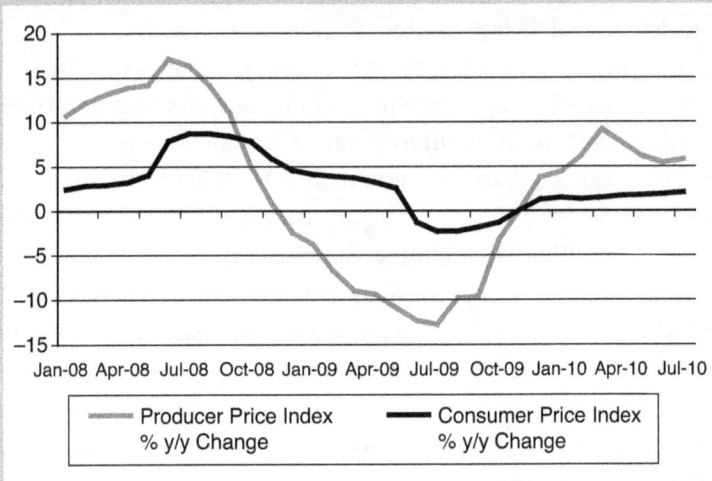

Figure 3. Trends in PPI and CPI Growth

In summary, the projected growth in Malaysia in the short run is supported by the following: First, private consumption and investment are supported by strengthened consumer and investor confidence and improved employment conditions. Second, there is increasing external support from gradual recovery in global demand and continuing exports to Asia, especially China and other emerging markets. Third, the ample liquidity will continue to drive recovery as monetary policies in 2010 remain accommodative and fiscal policies in 2011 remain growth-centred. Fourth, the uptrend in investment from both domestic and foreign sources may result from improving investor confidence and sentiments especially if the ongoing structural reforms and market liberalization measures are sustained.

Supported by the expectations of stronger investment flows and efficiency gains from structural reforms and policy changes, the long term growth forecast from 2012 to 2020 is projected to rise by 0.5–5 per cent per annum. Prospects for long-term economic growth are supported by the likelihood that the economy will become less vulnerable to the world trade cycle and fluctuations in global demand, as more resources will be devoted to the development of new, higher-value services. Ongoing efforts by the government to facilitate the expansion of the services sector will support Malaysia's long-term growth. These efforts will reduce the country's dependence on the manufacture of electronic and electrical goods. Malaysia will also continue to play a leading role in the development of Islamic banking and finance.

Key Risks and Challenges

In the short term, the global recovery is proving to be more fragile than expected, due to severely weakened financial structures in advanced economies, threat of deflation in Japan, and high unemployment rates in the European Union and United States and unsustainable fiscal deficits. Structural reforms, particularly through the removal of subsidies, may adversely affect domestic consumption

Malaysia: Selected Economic Indicators, 2005–2012F

	2005	2006	2007	2008	2009	2010E	2011F	2012F
GDP growth (% change)	5.3	5.8	6.5	4.7	-1.7	6.8	4.2	4.7
— Industry sector growth (% change)	3.5	4.5	3.0	0.8	-7.0	8.5	4.0	4.2
— Service sector growth (% change)	7.3	7.5	10.3	7.5	2.6	6.0	4.5	5.3
— Agricultural sector growth (% change)	2.6	5.2	1.3	4.3	0.4	4.0	2.3	2.5
Exports (US$ billion)	141.0	160.7	176.1	199.5	157.4	190.9	210.0	223.0
Imports (US$ billion)	114.6	131.2	146.9	156.9	123.8	156.3	171.1	184.1
Trade balance (US$ billion)	33.2	37.4	37.2	51.3	40.3	43.0	48.2	48.8
Current account balance (% of GDP)	14.5	16.7	15.7	17.5	17.7	14.7	15.1	13.5
Inflation/CPI average (% change)	3.0	3.6	2.0	5.4	0.6	1.8	2.7	3.2
M2 monetary supply growth (% change)	15.4	16.6	11.0	13.3	9.5	9.4	9.8	14.0
Fiscal balance (as % of GDP)	-3.6	-3.3	-3.2	-4.8	-7.0	-5.3	-4.9	-4.6
Total debt outstanding (US$ billion)	52.0	55.0	61.6	66.2	58.8	61.7	62.5	64.5
Long-term debt (US$ billion)	38.8	43.2	38.5	43.4	39.6	38.0	38.4	40.3
Debt service ratio (as % of exports)	5.6	4.0	4.8	3.6	5.8	4.6	3.7	2.9
Foreign exchange reserves (US$ billion)	69.9	82.1	101.0	91.1	95.4	97.5	103.2	111.1
Exchange rate at year-end (S$/US$1)	3.78	3.53	3.31	3.46	3.42	3.25	3.22	3.23

NOTE: E refers to estimates; F refers to forecasts.
SOURCE: Economist Intelligence Unit.

behaviour and cause unexpected inflationary pressure which may dampen growth. With a relatively healthy financial sector and high interest differentials between Malaysia and advanced economies, capital flows are expected to increase that might cause significant volatility in the exchange rate, which will affect the performance of export-oriented sectors.

Consumer and investor confidence remains a key factor in the short term. Over the medium- to long-term horizon, the increases in total factor productivity are indispensable for sustainable economic growth. To sustain a GDP growth of 6–7 per cent, which is required to achieve the goal of becoming a high-income economy by 2020, an average of 2 per cent growth in total productivity is needed. As a result, international competitiveness and long-term upgrading of more industries are key challenges in the longer term.

In Malaysia, the major obstacles to economic progress and higher productivity are inadequate numbers of highly educated and highly skilled personnel in the workforce. A shortage of skilled labour impedes progress at the upper end of the value chain. A positive discrimination in favour of bumiputra (ethnic Malays and other indigenous peoples) may continue to hamper labour market efficiency.

Malaysia's membership of ASEAN puts it in a good position to take advantage of an increase in intra-Asian trade. However, China's growing economic dominance within the region may eventually begin to cause problems for Malaysia as competition for resources grows.

In the long term, an unreceptive domestic economy to structural reforms (weak or derailed implementation of structural reforms) will hamper growth, through weaker consumer sentiments and less-than-aggressive investment behaviour. With the effects of free trade agreements felt in the domestic economy, slow upgrading and misallocation of resources to relatively less-cost-efficient industries can erode overall national competiveness and inevitably lead to a long-term decline.

Myanmar

Thein Swe

The Union of Myanmar has been implementing National Development Plans with a series of short-term economic plans. The present fourth short-term Five Year Plan (2006–07 to 2010–11), which will end in March 2011, has been formulated to achieve an average growth rate of 12 per cent annually. Myanmar expects the economic growth of FY2010, the fourth year of the Fourth Five Year Plan, to be 12 per cent compared to 10.1 per cent in FY2009, mainly due to increasing export earnings from gas and agriculture exports. According to the Governor of Myanmar at the International Monetary Fund (IMF) and World Bank Annual Meeting, the contributing factors for these high growth rates are due to favourable weather conditions that have led to higher agricultural production (mainly exports of rice, beans, and pulses), and to new gas fields and other natural resources in mining with strong export sectors.[1]

According to another report from the Asian Development Bank (ADB)'s *Asian Development Outlook (ADO) 2010 Update* of September 2010, Myanmar's GDP growth is however expected to rise to 5 per cent in FY2010 (ending 31 March 2011) and to 5.3 per cent in FY2011. As such, the official GDP growth rates are much higher than these unofficial ADB estimates. Since 2003, the ADB has indicated

MYANMAR

- Growth is expected to get a lift from foreign investment in new gas fields and the construction of an oil and gas pipeline to China.

- Agricultural production, especially rice, is expected to increase further.

- Rising private consumption, with public consumption and investment also likely to rise due to expenditure related to national elections.

- Inflation is forecast to rise due to rising costs of imported goods and fuel.

- Current account is forecast to widen.

that "an objective assessment of economic developments in Myanmar is made difficult by poor quality data. Often, information is available only with a long lag, is incomplete, and is difficult to reconcile" (*ADO* 2003). Also in the *ADO 2010 Update*, it has indicated that the data are inconsistent with variables closely correlated with economic growth, such as energy use and fertilizer applications. Similarly, other international institutions have also made their own estimates, such as the IMF and London-based Economist Intelligence Unit (EIU).

The ADB has projected the economy to grow this year from two large investments from China: new gas fields and construction of an oil and gas pipeline. Private consumption will also increase from an increase in public sector wages announced earlier in the year, and with higher rural incomes from a modest increase in agricultural commodity prices and a gradual increase in agricultural production. Public consumption and investment are likely to rise due to expenditure related to national elections conducted on 7 November 2010. In FY2011, the agricultural output is projected to increase further if more efforts are made to modernize the sector after the elections. Inflation is forecast to be around 7.5 per cent in FY2010 as prices for imported food and fuel rise from last year's low levels. Increases in the value of exports during the period will have to make up for the increase in imports due to higher prices for imported petroleum products and increased imports of capital equipment, construction materials, and consumer goods. According to ADB's *Asian Development Outlook 2010 Update*, the current account deficit has widened from 1.6 per cent of GDP in FY2010 to 2.3 per cent in FY2011. The IMF (*World Economic Outlook*, October 2010) has projected the current account deficit to widen in 2010 to 2.4 per cent of the GDP and 2.3 per cent of GDP in 2011.

The IMF has projected a growth rate of 5.3 per cent for 2010 and 5 per cent for 2011 for Myanmar.[2] Although in the previous year, the IMF projected a pick up in growth, it has projected a slight slowdown for 2011 and the following year. The EIU *Country Report* on Myanmar in September 2010, on the other hand, estimated growth of up to 4 per cent, mainly due to investment in energy and petroleum projects, especially from China. Excluding these sectors, the economy is projected to be sluggish. But it recognized the rebound in agriculture, which was seriously affected by Cyclone Nargis in the rice growing area of Ayeyawaddy (Irrawaddy) division in 2008. Although growth was partly due to favourable weather conditions, more needs to be done in terms of increase in agricultural investment to speed up agriculture production with crucial equipment and inputs.

The manufacturing sector is also facing challenges in obtaining the required investments and inputs, and at the same time facing weak external demand from the export-oriented firms, partly due to economic sanctions from western countries. However, according to a recent issue of *Seven Weekly* news magazine, garment factories have received orders on a piecework basis for payment up to December 2010, according to the Myanmar Garment Manufacturers' Association. "In previous years, our industry was busy from June to September when overseas commodity orders came to us. Beyond this period, we did not receive garment orders. We had to hope for these orders from foreign countries for the remaining period. At present, we have received more garment orders of foreign clients, especially from Japan and Korea", said a responsible person of the Myanmar Garment Manufacturers' Association. This is partly due to stricter labour laws in China. Some Japanese buyers have made garment orders with Myanmar garment factories for 2010 and discussions are ongoing to finalize new contracts for 2011. However, there could be labour shortage as many Myanmar workers are working at garment factories along the Myanmar-Thai border areas where they can earn higher wages.

The budget deficits financed through the Central Bank was the root cause of the high inflationary environment for many years since 2002, when the IMF estimated an inflation rate of over 58 per cent. Then the rate gradually came down to 26.3 per cent in 2006 and rose again to nearly 33 per cent in 2007. When fuel prices were again increased after an earlier increase in 2005, the continued budget deficits and the increase in fuel prices of petrol, diesel, and gas pushed up general consumer prices. The inflation rate in 2007 rose again to nearly 33 per cent. This growing inflation resulted in a drastically high cost of living and hardship for the citizens. It led to protests from large segments of the affected civilians as well as monks, with subsequent bloodshed and arrests.

Also according to the ADB, the budget deficits financed by the Central Bank also led to money supply M2 to increase to over 27 per cent in 2006 and to 30 per cent in 2007 when fuel prices in the country were increased by around 800 per cent. It gradually came down to 22.5 per cent in 2008, and again around to only 8 per cent in 2009. The IMF has projected an increase to around 9 per cent in 2010 and a slight increase to 9.2 per cent and more in 2011 and beyond. Moreover, some construction projects of the government have been completed and the budgets are decreasing. This is also due to the government policy of privatization, where a number of state-owned enterprises have been sold to the private sector, and money supply has contracted significantly in the private sector. Similarly, new banking licences were issued recently to businesses with close links to the regime. Concerns have been expressed over the sudden rush of the regime, on the eve of the elections, to sell off tranches of state assets and enterprises. About 300 enterprises and properties have been sold, including ports, rice mills, cigarette and textile factories, cinemas, hotels, an airline, fish and agricultural processing plants, and ruby, jade, and gold mines. Sales included vacant government buildings which had been used by ministries and departments that have since been relocated to Naypyidaw, the new capital of the country.

Myanmar has been using a multiple exchange-rate regime. The official exchange rate coexists or is in parallel with informal market rates. The official exchange rate is pegged at kyats 8.50847 per SDR (special drawing rights) since 1977, although its valuation is allowed to differ within a range of 2 per cent. However, the informal market rate has been the one used by the private sector. By 2006, the rate was more than K1,300/USD. According to EIU estimates, kyats to U.S. dollars gradually decreased to around K1,055/USD by 2009. Although EIU, in September 2010, projected the rate to be around K1,120/USD, the kyat has strengthened in the informal market to around K890/USD by end October 2010, and is expected to stay around this rate for some time. This is also in line with the appreciation of the national currencies in many of the Southeast Asian countries, mainly due to the depreciation of the U.S. dollar.

However, the closing of the border between Myawaddy in Myanmar and Mae Sot, Thailand had a huge impact on many businesses and further caused the appreciation of the kyat. Apart from the slowdown in the economy and border trade, scarcity of the kyat in circulation has been another reason for the appreciation of the kyat. It is also due to the government's increased tax rates, collection of fines for unlicensed vehicles, and for issuing licences, auctions of illegal vehicles, and privatization of state enterprises and assets as indicated earlier. At the same time, the fall in value of the U.S. dollar and foreign exchange earnings in Myanmar during FY2010 have considerably affected the export sectors of the economy.

In 1993, Foreign Exchange Certificates (FECs) were introduced at a fixed rate of one FEC to one U.S. dollar, via licensed exchange counters. The government issued the FECs initially to promote tourism. But in the informal market, the conversion rates were slightly different. During the first half of 2010, the exchange rate between the FEC and the U.S. dollar was almost the same as when it was first introduced in 1993. Although the rate was around K1,055 to US$1, the FEC was selling at a much higher rate than U.S. dollars due to its usefulness in paying rental charges and telephone and other utility bills by foreign companies and international NGOs, as required. The FEC could also be utilized to purchase fuel from the gas stations. Now with private gas stations and available pre-paid phone cards, FEC's usefulness has become limited. Another reason, if not the main reason, was a rumour that under the new financial policy, FECs may be terminated after the November 2010 elections. The current system of multiple exchange rates that is non-transparent creates distortions and higher costs. After the November 2010 elections, the new government should consider unification of the rates which would benefit the country from more efficient allocation of resources.

Regarding the external sector, export revenue is expected to grow in 2011 to about US$8 billion. Revenue from the sale of natural gas will remain high especially with new fields coming into operation. Revenue from rice, pulses and beans, and timber will also strengthen with recovery in regional demand due to an increase in economic growth, and the free trade agreements which became effective from the beginning of January 2010 between ASEAN countries and China, India, Japan, South Korea, Australia, and New Zealand. Similarly, imports are expected to rise from around US$4 billion to around US$5 billion and over in the next one or two years. But trade surplus is expected to continue at around US$3 billion that would lead to further current account surplus that would result in further addition to the country's foreign exchange reserve. This is projected to increase to over US$6 billion in 2010, to over US$8 billion in 2011, and could reach US$10 billion by 2012 when many of the gas and energy projects come on stream.

Although economic sanctions have been imposed by the United States, the European Union, Australia, and Japan, especially new U.S. sanctions targeting the assets of the country's leaders, and stricter controls on U.S. exports to Myanmar, these measures have not been effective. The sanctions are definitely affecting the people but do not affect the government as long as the three neighbouring countries — China, India, and Thailand — continue to have extensive business relations with Myanmar.

By the end of FY2009, 52 per cent of Myanmar's exports went to Thailand as a top export destination, followed by India with 17 per cent, and China with nearly 10 per cent in the third position — i.e., nearly 80 per cent of exports went to these three countries. The primary sources of imports are also mainly from these countries, at around 56.3 per cent of overall imports. If Singapore was added, it was nearly 74 per cent of overall imports. Hence, during the press conference in late October 2010, the Minister of Agriculture and Irrigation said that sanctions were no obstacles to trade and that there is no need to ask for the lifting of the sanctions as the government is already making them ineffective. According to the Central Statistical Organization (CSO) of the Ministry of National Planning and Economic Development, total foreign direct investment (FDI) in Myanmar was over $16 billion as of end March 2010. Thailand, the United Kingdom, China, Singapore and Malaysia are the major investing countries in Myanmar and there are now 63 Chinese firms investing in Myanmar.

In May 2010, US$8.173 billion of new FDI was recorded, boosting the total contracted FDI since 1988 by more than 50 per cent. This new FDI was spread across four projects in the oil and gas, electric power, and mining sectors, with the two power investments coming from mainland China, and mining and oil and gas FDI from Hong Kong. These are figures according to the CSO. The projects are believed to be for two hydropower dams in Kachin State, valued collectively at US$5.030 billion; China National Petroleum Corporation's oil and natural gas pipeline from Rakhine State to Yunnan Province (US$2.146 billion); and Norinco's planned development of the Letpadaung copper deposit near Monywa (US$997 million).

In early September 2010, China also provided an interest-free loan of US$4 billion according to an Asia News report. The *Bangkok Post* on 29 July 2010 reported that Thailand was to sign an agreement on 30 July 2010. It would be a thirty-year agreement with Myanmar to purchase gas from Zawtika field in Myanmar and the gas would come on stream from 2013. This deal will also lengthen the existing Trans-ASEAN gas pipeline from the current 2,800 kilometre to 3,020 kilometre and help ensure energy security in the ASEAN region. Again, during the recent visit to Myanmar by Prime Minister Abhisit of Thailand, an agreement was signed for Thai firms to build a deep-sea port in Tanintharyi (Tenasserim) region in Myanmar with a transport link to Thailand. The agreement included the construction of a 160 kilometre road, and rail links between Kanchanaburi in western Thailand with the port of Dawei (Tavoy). A special economic zone is also to be built on the 40,500 hectare land near the port.

The transport links, power plants, and steel mills that will be part of the project are expected to cost more than US$13 billion, the largest single investment in Myanmar, according to the *Financial Times'* Bangkok correspondent. Vessels bound for Thailand, China, Vietnam, and Laos could cut an average of ten days from their voyages, avoid the need to pass through the historically well-known pirate lair of the Malacca Strait, and make the voyages more secure by using this road and port.

Similarly, the Chinese project of constructing railways and motorways from Kyaukphyu to Shweli will be carried out in phases. The routes are the initial ones from Rakhine State to China. Kyaukphyu region will be like a commercial hub in Rakhine State. At present, real estate prices have tripled compared with those of the past five years. Myanmar and China are also in the midst of discussions to build Kyaukphyu deep-sea port. Kyaukphyu will become not only a main oil exporting sea port, but also a special commercial zone.

Presently, the Myanmar diaspora abroad, skilled and unskilled, are doing well in different fields, and many intellectuals are in such fields as chemical engineering, electrical engineering, medicine, law, and business to name a few. Many might not want to return because of the lack of opportunities and freedom of choice. For the past several decades, there seems to have been an exodus, not only of the young generation but also of educated middle-aged people, contributing their knowledge, skills, and experiences to their adopted countries.

But there are many willing to come back to their motherland if they are encouraged by governments like India. Many have also returned partly due to economic recession in their adopted countries. Such occurrences in Myanmar could be a kind of brain transfusion instead of brain drain from the country. The country does need much brain transfusion and it is important for the elected government, after the November 2010 elections, to take heed and encourage many of the interested and willing diaspora to return, in order that the country can realize its full potential in the global environment.

Unfortunately, Myanmar at present is still a poor developing country with the lowest per capita income in the Greater Mekong Subregion of peninsular Southeast Asia. A joint United Nations Development Programme and Government of Myanmar Integrated Household Living Conditions Assessment (2007) places poverty incidence at 32 per cent, with rural poverty significantly higher at 36 per cent compared with urban poverty at 22 per cent. In the last *Human Development Index 2009* released by UNDP, the country was ranked 138 out of 182 countries.

Myanmar's first national elections in twenty years were held on 7 November 2010. But it will take a very committed new government to turn around from the greedy cronies and regime-friendly foreign investors continuing to exploit the vast natural resources of the country. However, there are others who are more positive and believe that in the short term there will be little change economically, but do believe that once the administrative structures are in place, including in the states and regions (divisions), there will be more autonomy with also economic change emerging on the ground. But the relationships between the central and the local/regional authorities, including the ethnic indigenous peoples, will be crucial for political and economic improvement and the development of the country.

Recently, at a seminar in Yangon, a former senior UN official and also a Myanmar economist said that the health care, education, and welfare sectors should be accorded priority in terms of reforms after the elections. He urged more transparency in the country's development process. He mentioned the need for decision makers and business circles to be ethical and be held accountable to the public. He also urged the establishment of Corporate Social Responsibility (CSR) in Myanmar to make the business community more ethical. CSR is also crucial for the social and economic development of the whole country.

Myanmar's 2010 elections will also be considered by the neighbouring countries as challenges and opportunities in their relations with the country. Although there are diverse opinions that the elections will be neither free nor fair, they are likely to accept any poll result that does not involve major instability in the region. The release of Daw Aung San Suu Kyi after the election would be an opportunity for the new government to move forward with national reconciliation. And sometimes there may be a need to agree to disagree but to work together for the good of all the people of the country. Myanmar is a country with abundant natural resources. The increasing energy and other natural resource needs by neighbouring countries and their business could come into play with the divergent interests of individuals and business and with the policy implementation of neighbouring national and local governments. However, Myanmar should not waste these opportunities but optimize the environment for the economic development of the country, making sure it avoids a resource curse or Dutch disease and the subsequent loss of another generation.

NOTES

1. Statement by the Governor of the Bank for Myanmar at the 2010 Annual Meeting of the International Monetary Fund and the World Bank Group, Washington D.C. Press Release No. 7, 8 October 2010. Myanmar Millennium Development Goals Report 2006, Ministry of National Planning and Economic Development, Myanmar.
2. Although there have been no transactions with the government since 1988, under Article IV of its Articles of Agreement, the IMF has a mandate to exercise surveillance over the economic, financial, and exchange rate policies of its members in order to ensure the effective operation of the international monetary system. The Executive Board of IMF concluded the 2009 Article IV consultation with Myanmar on 24 February 2010 (Press Release No. 10/87, 12 March 2010). The World Bank staff usually joins in the IMF missions.

The Philippines

Aladdin D. Rillo

As in the past, growth in domestic output will continue to be driven by private consumption. Private consumption will expand by 5 per cent from 4.8 per cent a year ago, in line with improvements in remittances

---

THE PHILIPPINES

- After growing rapidly by 7.2 per cent in 2010, growth is likely to return to trend in 2011. Real GDP growth will moderate to 5.1 per cent due to slower global growth and normalization of stimulus measures.

- Based on momentum, however, the Philippines still has the capacity to reach its potential provided that appropriate policy measures are implemented to address capacity constraints and output gaps.

- The Philippines can also take advantage of the optimism brought by the new political leadership to sustain investor confidence and restore productive investments that have eluded the country for many years now.

and incomes. Remittances, which account for 10 per cent of GDP, are projected to further increase this year as recovery around the world continues. The gradual decline in unemployment (6.9 per cent as of July 2010, from 7.6 per cent a year ago) is also positive for private consumption, in addition to the positive impact of government cash transfer measures to support the low-income groups. Current efforts under the Aquino administration to focus on social services and infrastructure will also support increases in disposable income that can enhance private spending especially in the rural areas.

Despite a slowdown in global trade, exports of goods and services will remain an important source of growth. The Philippines is one of the most dependent countries on advanced markets for its exports, hence a slowdown in these markets will definitely hurt export revenues this year. However, increasing demand for exports in fast growing markets like China and India can help cushion the reduction in demand from traditional export markets like the United States, Europe, and Japan. The planned expansion in some export sectors is also likely to boost output. For example, in the electronics sector, an annual investment inflow of US$2 billion in the sector is expected starting this year, in line with the objective of generating export revenues of US$50 billion by 2016.

As some fiscal stimulus measures are rolled back, public consumption is likely to slow down to 3.7 per cent before finally picking up again to 4.6 per cent in 2012, as the government infrastructure programme gets fully under way. Under the public-private partnership (PPP) initiative for infrastructure — which the Aquino administration has made a centrepiece programme given its revenue woes and lack of infrastructure in the country — around eighty projects worth US$17.2 billion will be undertaken in the next six years (2011–16). A short list of ten PPP infrastructure projects worth US$2.9 billion is expected to be implemented this year, to be financed mainly by bond issuance. Obviously this will help boost construction activity, thus adding more to domestic output. However, the increasing trend in government spending also suggests a bigger budget deficit this year

(3.6 per cent of GDP) than targeted by the government (3.3 per cent of GDP).

One downside to output growth is the continued weakness in private investments, which are not expected to pick up strongly this year given the ongoing concerns regarding the overall business environment. Although capacity utilization is recovering in line with the expected boom in the construction industry and business sentiment has risen (due to maintenance of low inflation and interest rates in the country), it would take more than the usual government incentives and business promotions to address the declining investment-to-GDP ratio in the country. According to the 2011 *Doing Business Report* by the International Finance Corporation, the Philippines further slipped in ranking in terms of ease of doing business, from 144th place (out of 183 economies) in 2009 to 148th place in 2010. Among the biggest roadblocks for business identified in the report are the processes involved in starting a business and securing construction permits, in which the Philippines ranked 156th place in both categories.

On the supply side, the services sector (55 per cent of GDP) is expected to continue driving the economy to a higher growth path, given the bright prospects for the business process outsourcing (BPO) industry. After generating revenues of US$9.5 billion last year, the BPO industry is expected to expand further to US$12 billion this year; and possibly growing by 128 per cent a year over the next twelve years. Growth will be strong in back-office services such as publishing, finance, corporate services, and creative services. According to a recent survey conducted by the Business Processing Association of the Philippines, the majority of firms indicated that their companies will grow by about 50 per cent in the next twelve months in virtually every value-added sector. The International Monetary Fund (IMF) also projected growth in the BPO to accelerate in the coming years, and to become a key growth driver in the country.

After a dry spell that brought a disappointing growth last year (–2.0 per cent), the agriculture sector is expected to rebound in 2011, growing by 3.3 per cent. Recovery will be facilitated by distribution of quality breed stock that will boost the sector's productivity, as well as by increased agricultural lands (two million hectares) being created under the country's medium-term agricultural development plan. If the country is successful in embarking on complementary industries such as power and irrigation projects, it is likely that the sector will benefit from increased foreign investments in agriculture. For example, a number of countries, including South Korea, Qatar, Saudi Arabia, Bahrain, and Kuwait, have already expressed interest to invest in the country's agriculture sector over the next five years. Obviously these developments are positive for a sector that accounts for 20 per cent of domestic output and employs more than half of the country's workforce. Meanwhile, growth in industrial output (4.6 per cent) is likely to remain modest due to a weak performance of the manufacturing sector. In a study conducted by Mercer in 2008, poor business infrastructure, relatively higher labour costs, and falling labour productivity have been identified as key factors that contributed to the decline of the country's competitive advantage. Despite government efforts to address these issues, the contribution of the manufacturing sector to overall output growth has remained limited over the years.

In line with volatile external conditions, the country's external balances are expected to moderate but will continue to be robust. Although merchandise exports with other emerging markets like China, India, and ASEAN are likely to increase compared to previous years, this will not be enough to offset the decline in exports from advanced markets. As a result growth in merchandise exports will slow to 12 per cent from 22 per cent a year ago. Growth in merchandise imports will also moderate but not by as much (16 per cent), given the increased demand for intermediate inputs to support the country's infrastructure projects and higher import payments generated by rising oil prices. As imports outpace exports, a higher trade deficit of US$14.8 billion is expected. However, with increasing capital inflows and steady remittances, the current account will remain in surplus, albeit lower, at 3.9 per cent of GDP. Reflecting this, the international reserves will rise further to US$54.8 billion by year-end as the peso consolidates at PhP42.1 against the U.S. dollar.

Monetary conditions are also expected to remain accommodative. With the inflation rate contained at 4.1 per cent, which is within the inflation target (3–5 per cent) set by the Bangko Sentral ng Pilipinas (central bank or BSP), it is likely that a tightening will only occur towards the second half of the year, possibly a rate hike of 50 basis points. In line with the benign inflation and tentative recovery in real output, liquidity growth (M2) is projected at 14.4 per cent, and any significant growth in liquidity is not envisaged unless there are compelling signs of weakness in the economy and incipient pressures in prices become entrenched. Private credit growth is also projected to be more accommodating as banks focus their activities more on retail financial products and as the government provides more opportunities in the countryside. On the fiscal side, the real challenge is to rationalize spending and focus on increasing tax efforts as the government aims to gradually reduce the budget deficit to 2 per cent of GDP by 2013.

In line with the continuation of the global recovery, economic prospects in the Philippines will remain favourable in 2011. However, given the country's history of unstable growth, it is crucial that the momentum is sustained by focusing on key priority areas to support growth in the near term.

First there is an urgent need to increase the levels of private investments in the country, particularly foreign direct investments (FDI) that can provide a strong anchor for growth. Since the 1997/98 crisis, aggregate investment — particularly private fixed investment — has failed to recover to the pre-crisis (i.e., before 1997) level and has remained low for more than a decade now. While the factors that have held back investment in the country are well known (e.g., low returns and greater uncertainty in doing business), it is about time that policies are directed seriously to addressing these issues, with clear commitment and credible actions from the policymakers. Establishing a clear framework for businesses to operate will be crucial, including putting in place the appropriate

Philippines: Selected Economic Indicators, 2006–2012F

	2006	2007	2008	2009	2010E	2011F	2012F
GDP growth (%)	5.3	7.1	3.7	1.1	7.2	5.1	5.4
— Private Consumption	5.5	5.9	4.7	4.1	4.8	5.0	5.1
— Public Consumption	10.4	6.6	0.4	10.9	7.9	3.7	4.6
— Gross Fixed Invest	3.9	10.9	2.7	-0.4	11.3	4.4	4.7
Exports (US$ million)	46,526	49,512	48,253	37,610	46,033	51,757	58,164
Imports (US$ million)	53,258	57,903	61,138	46,473	57,391	66,573	70,855
Trade Balance (US$ million)	-6,732	-8,391	-12,885	-8,863	-11,358	-14,816	-12,691
Current Account (% GDP)	4.5	4.9	2.2	5.5	4.4	3.9	4.0
CPI Inflation (average; %)	6.2	2.8	9.3	3.2	3.9	4.1	4.4
M2 growth (end-period; %)	21.8	10.5	15.3	7.5	11.6	14.4	12.0
Interest Rate (average; %)*	5.1	5.0	5.1	4.2	4.1	4.4	4.7
Fiscal Balance (% GDP)**	-1.1	-0.2	-0.9	-3.9	-3.9	-3.6	-2.6
Public Debt (% GDP)	63.9	55.8	57.0	57.3	55.2	55.7	55.1
Ext Debt (% GDP)	50.5	38.1	32.3	32.8	30.8	27.6	25.4
Reserves (US$ million)	22,967	33,751	37,600	42,300	50,012	54,887	59,202
Exch Rate (end-period)	49.13	41.40	48.09	46.5	43.7	42.1	41.6

NOTES: E refers to estimates; F refers to forecasts; * 91-day T-bill rate; ** national government cash operations.
SOURCES: Country websites; EIU; Consensus Forecast Asia; author's estimates.

macroeconomic incentives and policies, investment climate, rule of law, and governance. But evidence of implementation is critical — and this is something that the country's policymakers must achieve. With the new political leadership, as well as renewed confidence in the country (as shown by recent upgrades on sovereign debt ratings), policymakers must be ready to level the playing field for the country's investors.

Second, credible and consistent macroeconomic policies matter. As concerns over the country's finances linger, serious considerations are needed to put the fiscal house in order. Obviously eliminating the fiscal deficit is difficult to achieve in the current environment of weak growth. However, this should not deter the authorities from addressing the key fiscal issues in the country such as weak tax efforts and inefficiencies in revenue collections. So far the current government is on the right track of making the improvements in public finances a priority. But more actions are needed. As mentioned in the *2010 Regional Outlook for the Philippines*, the immediate challenge is to implement reforms related to tax administration and enforcement of tax regulations, as well as measures to reform the power sector and accelerate privatization programmes. In addition to fiscal policy, credible measures to implement monetary policy, strengthen the financial sector, improve productivity, and encourage innovations are crucial for the Philippines.

Finally, sustaining the economic momentum for 2011 will only be as good as the political leadership that supports it. Time and again analysts have been convinced that the future of the Philippine economy does not lie solely on the number of economic measures being implemented, but more on the political will and commitment. The economic challenges facing the Aquino administration are nothing new, and the policies to address them are also not new. But a new political commitment — with new perspective and resolve — can make a big difference and change for the Philippine economy.

Singapore

Sng Hui Ying

Recent Economic Development

The Singapore economy entered into 2010 with the upward momentum that began in the middle of 2009, growing at a sizzling rate of 19.9 per cent and 18.8 per cent in the first and second quarter of 2010 on a year-on-year basis. The recovery of the economy from the late 2008 / early 2009 recession was as swift as the onslaught of the recession itself, giving rise to a "V-shaped" recovery (Figure 1). Growth has however moderated to an estimated 10 per cent in the third quarter of 2010 on a year-on-year basis. On a quarter-on-quarter basis, the Singapore economy suffered from a 19.8 per cent contraction in the third quarter. It is likely that growth has peaked and there could be further moderation ahead. In fact, the Singapore economy could enter into a technical recession in the second half of 2010 if the volatile biomedical cluster swings substantially negative and brings about another quarter-on-quarter contraction in the fourth quarter.

SINGAPORE

- The Singapore economy rebounded sharply from the 2008/09 recession, growing at 19.9 per cent and 18.8 per cent year-on-year in the first and second quarter of 2010.

- The economy showed signs of slowing down in Q3 2010, with GDP growth rate moderating to an estimated 10 per cent y/y for that quarter.

- Economic growth for the whole year of 2010 is forecast to be between 13 per cent and 15 per cent. GDP is projected to grow between 4.3 per cent and 5.3 per cent in 2011 and around 5 per cent in 2012.

- CPI inflation is expected to be 2.5–3 per cent in 2010 and 2–3 per cent in 2011.

- MAS further tightened Singapore's monetary policy in October 2010 to address the higher inflation risk. SGD is expected to strengthen against USD in the medium term.

Figure 1. "V-shaped" Recovery but Possible Slowdown Ahead

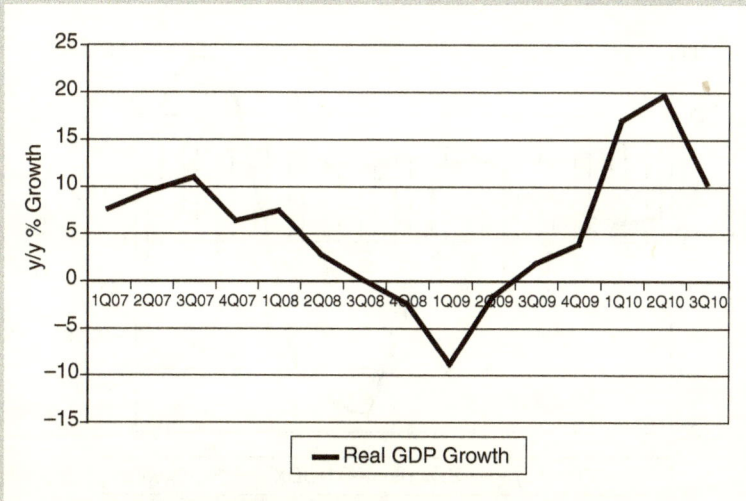

NOTE: 3Q 2010's figure is an advance estimate by MTI.
SOURCE: CEIC Database, www.singstat.com.sg.

The recovery of the Singapore economy was achieved on the back of the recovery of the global economy from the 2008/09 Great Recession. The International Monetary Fund (IMF) has forecast the world economy and all the major economies to achieve positive growth in 2010 and 2011. The positive development has translated to a sharp rebound in Singapore's exports. Total exports expanded by 28.2 per cent, 29.1 per cent, and 20.3 per cent on a year-on-year basis in the first, second, and third quarter of 2010 respectively, of which non-oil domestic exports (NODX) grew by 23.2 per cent, 27.6 per cent, and 23.8 per cent over the same period (Figure 2). Both electronic and non-electronic products contributed to the expansion of the NODX. The recovery of the exports sector was experienced across all major markets — European Union, United States, China, Hong Kong, and Malaysia all expanded significantly. The export market is expected to stay firm in the short run with holiday-season

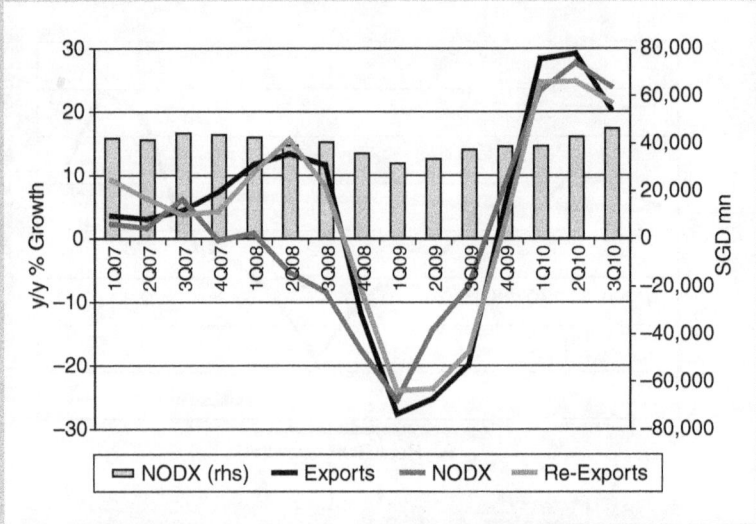

Figure 2. Sharp Recovery of the Export Sector

Source: CEIC Database.

inventory restocking taking place in the September to November period. Going ahead, however, Singapore's export growth is expected to moderate as consumer spending in developed countries sputters.

The sharp recovery of the NODX has in turn brought about an even sharper recovery of Singapore's manufacturing sector. The manufacturing sector, which was the villain in dragging the Singapore economy into a sudden contraction in late 2008 and early 2009, has contributed much to the V-shaped recovery of the Singapore economy in late 2009 and the first half of 2010, expanding by a remarkable 37.9 per cent and 44.5 per cent on a year-on-year basis in the first and second quarter of 2010 respectively (Figure 3). Growth was estimated to be a moderate 12.1 per cent in the third quarter of 2010 due to plant maintenance shutdowns and changes in value-mix of products of the pharmaceutical sector during the quarter.

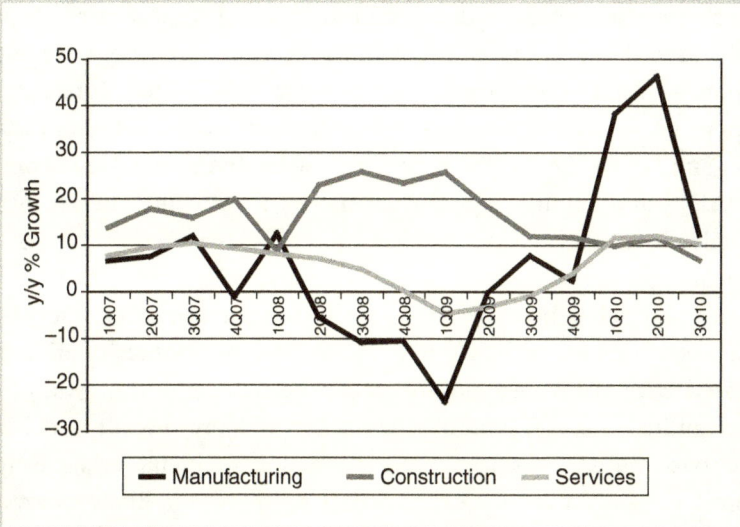

Figure 3. Booming Manufacturing Sector and Recovering Services Sector

NOTE: 3Q 2010's figure is an advance estimate by MTI.
SOURCE: CEIC Database.

The services sector, which underwent a gentler decline in late 2008 and entered a contraction in 2009, has also recovered, growing at a relatively slower but steady rate of 10 per cent year-on-year in the first three quarters of 2010 (Figure 3). The tourism sector was given a huge boost in 2010 when Singapore's two casino-based vacation resorts (officially known as integrated resorts), Resorts World Sentosa and Marina Bay Sands, officially opened. Visitor arrivals in Singapore have been steadily improving in 2010, with the number of visitor arrivals hitting a million in July 2010, a first in Singapore.

Growth of the construction sector, although still positive, was slowly declining (Figure 4). This was mainly due to the completion of key commercial and industrial building projects earlier in the year.

Economic Forecast

Looking ahead, positive factors such as continued growth in the global demand for electronic products and increasing visitor arrivals will provide growth support to Singapore's economy in the near term. Singapore's Ministry of Trade and Industry (MTI) has forecast the Singapore economy to grow at 13–15 per cent for the whole of 2010. This is similar to the 14 per cent forecast by the Asian Development Bank (ADB) and slightly higher than the 12.3 per cent forecast by the Economist Intelligence Unit (EIU).

The longer term outlook, however, is fraught with uncertainties, such as potential debt crises in some European countries, increasing risk of asset bubbles in many developing nations, global inflation risk associated with rising commodity prices, premature withdrawal of the fiscal stimulus packages, and over-extension of loose monetary policies. In the base case scenario where no major financial crisis erupts, economic activity in the major industrial economies is likely to expand at a slower pace due to the persistently high unemployment rates and fiscal consolidation in these countries. On the other hand, economic conditions in Asia, especially East Asia, are expected to stay strong. All these point to a slower but positive growth rate for Singapore in 2011 and 2012.

Singapore's GDP growth rate in 2011 is forecast to range between 4.3 and 5.29 per cent: 4.3 per cent (EIU), 5 per cent (ADB), and 5.29 per cent (IMF). The Monetary Authority of Singapore (MAS) expects the Singapore economy to expand at a more sustainable rate in line with its growth potential in 2011; Singapore's longer term sustainable growth rate is between 3 and 5 per cent. The growth rate in 2012 is forecast to be about 5 per cent in 2012; EIU's forecast is 5.1 per cent while the IMF's forecast is 5.07 per cent.

Inflation Outlook

In tandem with the global economy's brisk recovery from the 2008/09 recession, commodity prices have also started to increase. Commodities, in particular those that are in huge demand by the rapidly-growing China and India, are expected to experience continued upward pressure on their prices. Prolonged loose monetary policy and quantitative easing by central banks in the industrial countries could fuel further asset price inflation in the emerging economies. Going forward, the inflation risk faced by Singapore in the next two years is significant, but imported inflation could be moderate by an appreciating Singapore dollar.

Singapore's consumer price index (CPI) inflation rose significantly from 0.9 per cent in Q1 2010 to 3.1 per cent in Q2, and edged up further to 3.2 per cent in July–August (Figure 4). MAS expects the headline CPI inflation rate to rise to around 4 per cent by the end of 2010 and stay high in the first half of 2011 before moderating. Externally, food commodity prices and fuel prices have risen. Domestically, costs of accommodation and cars have increased. With the economy operating at close to full employment, labour cost is expected to increase and persist into 2011. The buoyant property market has also prompted the government to implement additional anti-speculation measures to

Figure 4. CPI Inflation Creeping Up

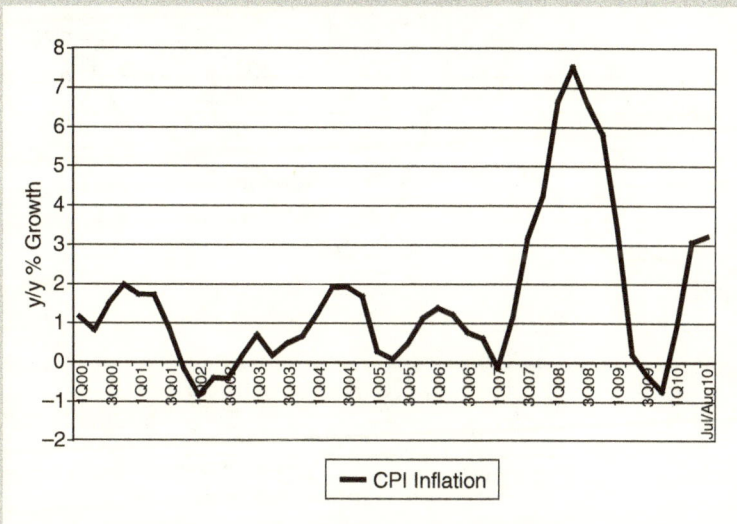

SOURCE: CEIC Database.

cool the property market in August 2010. This was the third attempt
to cool the property market since 2009.

MAS aims to cap CPI inflation at 2–3 per cent in 2011 from 2.5–
3 per cent in 2010 via tighter monetary policy.

Exchange Rate Policy

In April 2010, in view of the strong rebound of the Singapore economy
from the downturn and incipient inflationary pressures emanating from
domestic and external sources, MAS re-centred its exchange rate policy
band upward and shifted the policy band from that of a zero per cent
appreciation path to one of modest and gradual appreciation (Figure 5).
Partly due to the general weakness of the USD and partly due to the
appreciating path of the SGD, the SGD appreciated steadily against
the USD from 1.40/USD (0.714USD/SGD) at the beginning of 2010 to
around 1.29/USD (0.775USD/SGD) in mid-October 2010.

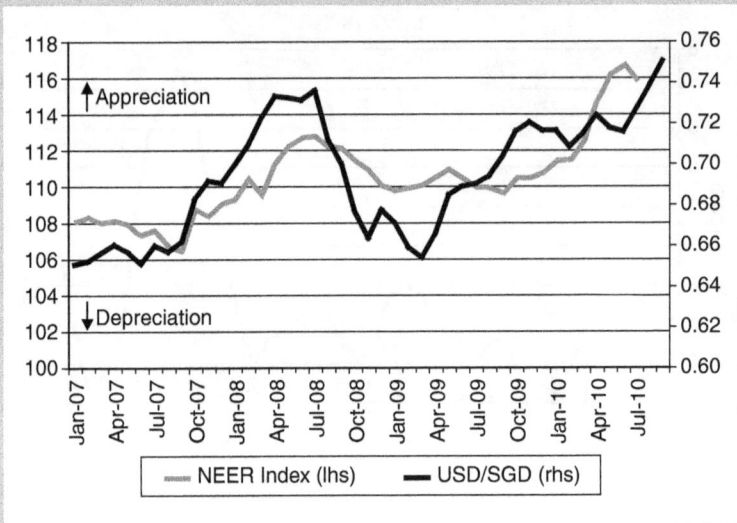

Figure 5. Strengthening SGD

Source: CEIC Database.

Singapore: Selected Economic Indicators, 2006–2012F

	2006	2007	2008	2009	2010E	2011F	2012F
GDP Growth (% change)	8.6	8.5	1.8	−1.3	12.3	4.3	5.1
— Industry Sector Growth (% change)	10.8	7.0	−1.0	−2.0	10.2	5.2	5.0
— Services Sector Growth (% change)	7.7	8.6	4.6	−1.4	13.2	3.9	5.1
Goods: Exports fob (US$ billion)	274.9	304.0	344.4	274.6	350.2	384.3	435.4
Goods: Imports fob (US$ billion)	232.1	256.9	313.5	241.1	310.0	338.7	389.2
Trade Balance (US$ billion)	42.8	47.1	30.9	33.5	40.1	45.7	46.2
Current Account Balance (% of GDP)	24.4	22.1	14.1	13.3	14.1	14.7	12.3
Inflation/CPI Average (% change)	1.0	2.1	6.6	0.6	2.6	2.0	1.5
M2 Money Supply Growth (% change)	19.4	13.4	12.0	11.3	10.2	12.0	13.5
Fiscal Balance (% of GDP)	0.5	3.1	1.4	−1.0	−2.7	−1.2	−0.2
Foreign Direct Investment (US$ billion)	27.7	31.6	22.7	19.6	21.0	23.9	25.1
Foreign Direct Investment (% of GDP)	19.1	17.8	11.8	10.7	9.7	10.2	10.0
Exchange Rate at Year-end (S$/US$1)	1.534	1.441	1.439	1.403	1.383	1.363	1.366

NOTES: E refers to estimates; F refers to forecasts.
SOURCE: Economist Intelligence Unit.

In the latest *MAS Monetary Policy Statement* announced on 14 October 2010, MAS weighted the balance of risks towards inflation after taking into consideration the continued expansion of the Singapore economy and rising pressure of domestic cost. MAS will continue with the policy of a modest and gradual appreciation of the S$NEER policy band in the next six months. The slope of the policy band will increase slightly, but the level at which the band is centred will remain unchanged. The policy band will be widened slightly in view of the volatility across international financial markets.

Thailand

Sakulrat Montreevat

The Thai economy is estimated to grow by 7 per cent in 2010, from a contraction of 2.2 per cent in 2009. This is attributed to the rebound in exports, which account for more than 60 per cent of Thai GDP. The rebound in export demand drove export-oriented manufacturing production and stimulated investment. Key challenges for policymakers were related to drought, pest outbreak, and political turmoil in the first half of 2010, and strong baht and flash floods in the second half of the year. However, the economy expanded at a

---

THAILAND

- Thailand faced challenges during 2010. However, the rebound in exports pulled the economy out of recession.

- Disbursement under the second stimulus package has been behind schedule. Questions remain over public infrastructure investment projects.

- The country's growth is forecast to slow down to 4–4.5 per cent in 2011–12. Challenges ahead include uncertainties in the global recovery and finance, political instability, the oil price hike, and unfavourable climate conditions.

high growth rate of 10.6 per cent in the first half of 2010. According to Thailand's Fiscal Policy Office (FPO), the strong baht and the floods in the second half of 2010 would not adversely affect GDP growth in 2010.

Facing growing budget pressures, the Abhisit government expects to return a balanced budget position by FY2015. Budgetary expenditure for FY2011 is set at 2.05 million baht, increasing by 16 per cent from that of FY2010. Of which, capital expenditure for FY2011 is 0.25 million baht, increasing by 40 per cent from that of 2010. Capital expenditure will be aimed at supporting the country's growth. Fiscal deficit is projected at 3.2 per cent of GDP in FY2011, down from 3.8 per cent in FY2010.

Thailand faces massive investment needs, as public investment has been depressed since the 1997–98 financial crisis. To enhance the country's competitiveness, the government aims to spur the economy through the Thai Khem Khaeng infrastructure investment programme (Second Stimulus Package: SP2) over the period 2010–12. However, disbursement of the SP2 funds which started in October 2009 was behind schedule. Accumulated disbursement at end-September 2010 amounted to 234.4 billion baht, or 67 per cent of the approved budget framework of 350 billion baht. Most of the financing for the SP2 is off-budget. As the off-budget is winding down, part of the SP2 will be transferred to the regular budget. Public debt declined to 43.2 per cent of GDP by June 2010, from 43.9 per cent at end-2009, providing room to borrow if the need arises.

According to the Finance Minister, the government will be investing 200 billion baht in several railway projects over the period 2011–15. This is significant if it is seen against the backdrop where the State Railway of Thailand has not made any real investments over the past sixty years. In October 2010, Parliament approved a draft framework for negotiations with China on a national high-speed train network project. The project would see China build five high-speed railway routes linking Bangkok to Nong Khai, Chiang Mai, Ubon Ratchathani, Rayong, and Padang Besar. Results of the negotiations with China would require parliamentary approval to move forward.

On the monetary policy front, the challenge for the Bank of Thailand (BOT) is to manage inflationary pressures as well as foreign capital flows to nurture the country's recovery. After the revival of the economy and with inflation on the rise in the first half of 2010, the BOT started to normalize the policy rate with increases in July and August 2010 of a cumulative 50 basis points to 1.75 per cent. Because of rising global uncertainty, the BOT in October 2010 decided to keep its policy rates unchanged at 1.75 per cent amid concerns that higher interest rates would attract even more foreign capital inflows.

A huge flux of foreign capital inflows into Thailand in 2010 put pressure on the baht to appreciate and on export products to be less competitive. The BOT allowed baht appreciation with intervention in July to September 2010, and introduced measures to encourage capital outflows in September 2010. However, the measures were unable to offset the large capital inflows into both the equity and bonds markets. In October 2010, the Cabinet approved the imposition of a 15 per cent tax for foreigners on bond-income earned, including interest income and capital gains. The baht appreciated about 10 per cent against the U.S. dollar during the first ten months of 2010 to 29.87/USD as of 1 November 2010. According to the Finance Minister, additional measures will be introduced if there is evidence of baht speculation. If the baht appreciates at a slower pace, the BOT could press ahead with its policy rate normalization.

Inflation averaged 3.4 per cent over the first nine months of 2010 as domestic demand and oil prices increased. Inflation is estimated at 3.5 per cent in 2010, from –0.9 per cent in 2009. This is due to the floods that occurred in the last quarter of 2010 that cut agricultural supplies and increased farm prices. With an assumption of an upward revision of the minimum wage and rising agricultural prices, the BOT expects higher inflation of 3 to 5 per cent in 2011.

On the production side, the drought and the pest outbreak in the first half of 2010 caused a fall in rice, oil palm, maize, and cassava production. Crop prices however continued to grow satisfactorily in response to favourable world demand. Manufacturing production was spurred by the growth in export demand. Production that expanded well in 2010 included vehicles, electrical appliances, and hard disk drives. Although the political turmoil happened in March–May 2010, tourism arrivals increased by 12.1 per cent in the first half of 2010. The unemployment rate in August 2010 was at 0.9 per cent of the total labour force. There were signs of labour shortages in some industries.

According to the FPO's early assessment, the floods in October 2010 ruined 2.4 million rai (384,000 hectares) of farmland. Factories in the textile, electronics, and auto industries also faced disruption. Tourism-related services, such as hotels and transport services, also suffered losses. The base-case damage was 11.9 billion baht, or 0.13 percentage points of GDP. The worst-case damage would be 20.21 billion baht, or 0.21 percentage points of GDP. The FPO projected that the Thai economy would expand at 7.3 per cent in 2010, taking into account the impact of baht volatility and floods. The country is forecast to grow at 4.5 per cent in 2011, assuming a rate of 30 baht to the U.S. dollar and favourable climatic conditions.

In July 2010, Thailand's National Economic and Social Development Board (NESDB) and the United Nations Development Programme (UNDP) began working in partnership to build a Creative Economy. The NESDB is to make the Creative Economy a pillar of its 11th National Economic and Social Development Plan (2012–16). Meanwhile, the UNDP will provide policy analysis and government expertise to assist the government in successfully transitioning the Thai economy. By creative industries, it is expected that more jobs and income will be generated. This will not only boost economic output, but will also provide greater opportunities to reduce social and economic inequalities.

Thailand: Selected Economic Indicators, 2006–2012F

	2006	2007	2008	2009P	2010E	2011F	2012F
GDP growth (% change)	5.1	4.9	2.5	-2.2	7.0	4.0	4.5
— Industry sector growth (% change)	5.8	6.1	3.8	-4.9	11.8	5.2	5.5
— Services sector growth (% change)	4.6	4.7	1.2	-0.3	3.8	3.2	3.9
— Agriculture sector growth (% change)	5.5	0.9	3.5	-0.5	2.5	2.2	2.5
Exports (US$ million)	127,941	151,258	175,233	150,743	188,429	211,040	242,696
Imports (US$ million)	126,947	138,476	175,604	131,355	178,118	201,629	237,923
Trade Balance (US$ million)	994	12,782	-371	19,388	10,311	9,411	4,773
Current account balance (% of GDP)	1.1	5.7	0.0	7.7	4.2	3.4	4.5
Inflation/CPI average (% change)	4.7	2.3	5.5	-0.9	3.5	4.0	4.2
M2 money supply growth (% change)	8.2	6.3	9.2	6.8	8.5	9.0	8.8
Fiscal Balance (as % of GDP)	0.1	-1.1	-0.3	-4.3	-3.8	-3.2	-2.5
Total external debt (US$ million)	59,643	74,416	76,102	83,911	65,000	67,000	70,000
Long term debt (US$ million)	41,089	40,400	42,498	43,904	40,820	42,076	43,960
Debt service ratio (% of exports)	11.4	11.8	7.1	6.7	2.2	6.8	7.1
International reserves (US$ million)	66,985	87,455	111,008	138,418	153,300	166,700	170,000
Exchange rate at year-end (Baht/US$1)	36.1	33.7	34.9	33.4	30.0	30.0	30.0

NOTES: P refers to preliminary; E refers to estimates; F refers to forecasts.
SOURCES: National Economic and Social Development Board, Bank of Thailand, Ministry of Finance, Economist Intelligence Unit, and author's estimation.

On the external front, Thailand is targeting average trade growth of 18–20 per cent a year with the member countries of ASEAN when the ASEAN Economic Community (AEC) comes into effect. The AEC's objective is to unite ASEAN member countries as a single market and production base for a comparative advantage for the region. ASEAN is now Thailand's largest trading partner. Two-way trade was worth US$49.21 billion in the first eight months of 2010, a 39.7 per cent year-on-year increase. Exports from Thailand to ASEAN member countries jumped 46 per cent to US$29.1 billion, while imports rose 31.5 per cent to US$20.11 billion.

Thailand's outward foreign direct investment (FDI) is growing. According to the United Nations Conference on Trade and Development, Thailand's outward FDI stock in 2009 stood at US$16 billion, 40 times its level in 1990. Based on the Stock Exchange of Thailand, Land & Houses leads local firms in terms of value of investment overseas, at US$344 million, followed by Delta Electronics, Saha-Union, Charoen Pokphand, and PTT Chemical. The Siam Cement Group (SCG) comes first in terms of overseas affiliates, followed by Charoen Pokphand, Minor International, Banpu, and Delta Electronics. The SCG, Thailand's top industrial conglomerate, plans to invest at least 100 billion baht over the period of 2011–15 to expand its businesses across ASEAN, including in two cement plants and acquisitions of paper and building-material factories.

The Thai economy is forecast to grow moderately to 4–4.5 per cent per year for 2011–12, given slow recovery of major trading partners, supportive fiscal policy, and flexible monetary policy. Inflation is projected to rise to 4–4.2 per cent per year due to an upward trend in the minimum wage, rising agricultural prices, and higher retail prices. The baht is expected to continue gaining, as the U.S. and EU governments are likely to extend monetary easing to stimulate their economic growth. Challenges to the economy over the forecast period include uncertainty in global recovery and finance, political instability, oil price hikes, and unfavourable climatic conditions.

Vietnam

Vu Minh Khuong

Vietnam today is more integrated into the world economy than most of its Asian peers on both trade and foreign direct investments (FDI) measures (Figure 1).

Behind Vietnam's impressive economic performance are its three major strengths. The first is related to the country's geographic and demographic advantages. The country is situated in the heart of Asia and borders China, a booming giant economy. With over 3,000 kilometres of coastline, the S-shaped country offers excellent conditions for all of its parts to participate in global trade. Furthermore, Vietnam is the world's thirteenth most populous country with a young population, which implies the country has both a large market and an energetic labour force. The second strength is its political stability. On the World Bank's indicator of "political stability", Vietnam ranks well above most of its Asian peers, including China, India, Malaysia, Indonesia, Thailand, and the Philippines. The country's third strength lies in its human capital. The Vietnamese people are known by many for their eagerness to improve their lives through hard work, their commitment to education, and their eagerness to seize emerging opportunities. Foreign investors have often praised Vietnamese workers for being quick-learning and industrious. As evidence, Vietnam is become among the top developing countries in adopting the Internet and sending students to study overseas.

VIETNAM

- Since launching its economic reforms in 1986, Vietnam has remarkably transformed itself from a country on the verge of economic collapse and isolation into one of the most open and fastest-growing economies in the world.

- The country has achieved rapid GDP growth with an average rate exceeding 7 per cent between 1990 and 2010.

- One of the main engines driving Vietnam's economic performance has been its robust integration into the world economy, with an average trade growth rate exceeding 20 per cent over the same period.

Figure 1. Global Integration: Vietnam vs. Asian Peers, 2008

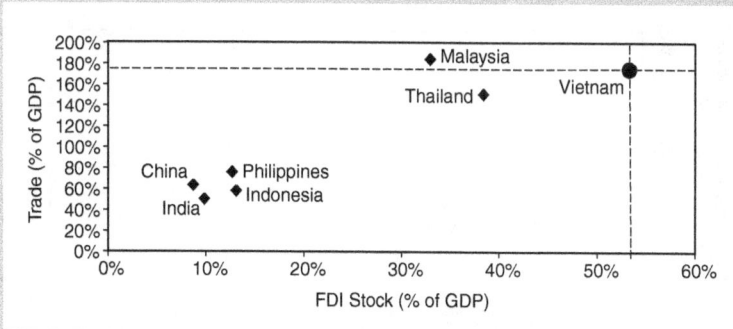

Source: World Bank and UNTAC.

Despite its remarkable progress on economic development over the past two decades, Vietnam is still significantly behind its Asian peers on the level of per capita income, and challenges ahead facing the economy remain formidable (Figure 2).

Development in Vietnam has been hindered by its three major weaknesses. The first is the country's lack of faithful commitment to free market principles. Although Vietnam has reaped immense benefits in shifting from a command to a market economy, it has been reluctant to make fundamental reforms to enable market forces to exert their full impacts. Unjustified subsidies and privileges provided to state-owned enterprises, large investments poured into commercially unviable projects, inadequate support for private sector development, and the persistence of "administrative control" attitudes (with effects across prices, exchange rates, and interest rates) have caused severe market distortions and investment inefficiencies in the economy.

The second weakness is about institutional building. While Vietnam has enjoyed rapid economic growth, its efforts to build good governance have been inadequate. The poor quality of public policy in the country, especially with regards to economic development, urban planning and management, corruption control, environmental protection, and education has become the main sources of society's concerns and disgruntlement. The rapid employment expansion of the government and

Figure 2. Income Level and Growth Performance: Vietnam vs. Peers

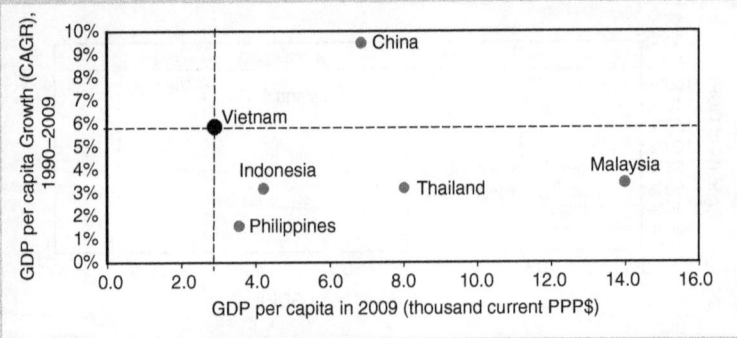

NOTE: GDP per capita growth (CAGR) for Cambodia is for the period 1993–2009.
SOURCE: World Development Indicators.

party-related sectors may have also been a factor that has deterred the country from improving its institutional competence and effectiveness. As shown in Figure 3, the labour productivity computed as value-added per employee has substantially deteriorated in the sectors associated with the government and the communist party.

Vietnam's third weakness is its leaning towards dependence on external resources. As a percentage of GDP, foreign aid and workers' remittances are much higher for Vietnam than for its Asian peers (Figure 4). With sizeable sources of foreign aid, the country tends to operate under the illusion of easy access to funding for grand projects, while paying insufficient attention to ensuring their economic efficiency and strategic effectiveness. In fact, the incremental capital-output ratio (ICOR) of Vietnam has risen sharply over time and exceeded the ratios observed for other developing Asian countries. That is, relative to its Asian peers, Vietnam has to invest more capital for one dollar increase in its GDP.

On the other hand, with large and increasing flows of workers' remittances, the country can enjoy rapid increases in consumption and impressive reductions in poverty without the pressing urgency for efforts to make people more productive and frugal. Vietnam's heavy dependence on foreign resources in fact has delayed the country's economic transformation towards structures of higher efficiency and productivity.

Figure 3. Labour Productivity Growth in Selected Sectors

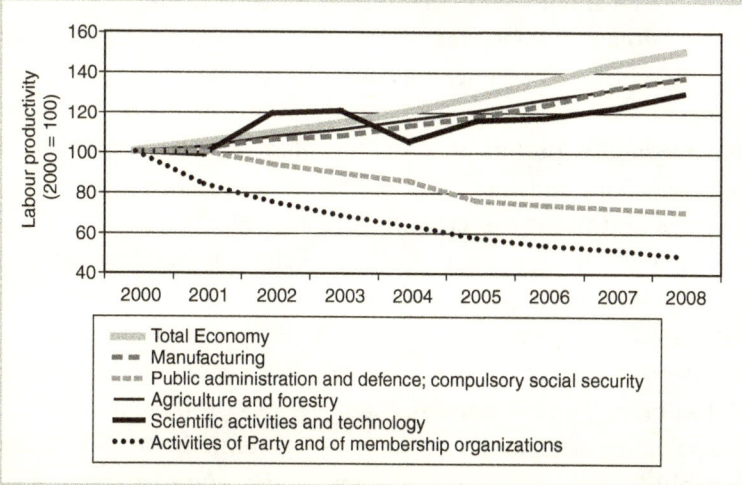

Legend:
- ▦▦ Total Economy
- – – Manufacturing
- ▪ ▪ Public administration and defence; compulsory social security
- —— Agriculture and forestry
- ▬▬ Scientific activities and technology
- •••• Activities of Party and of membership organizations

SOURCE: General Statistics Office, Vietnam.

Figure 4. External Resources Dependence, 2008

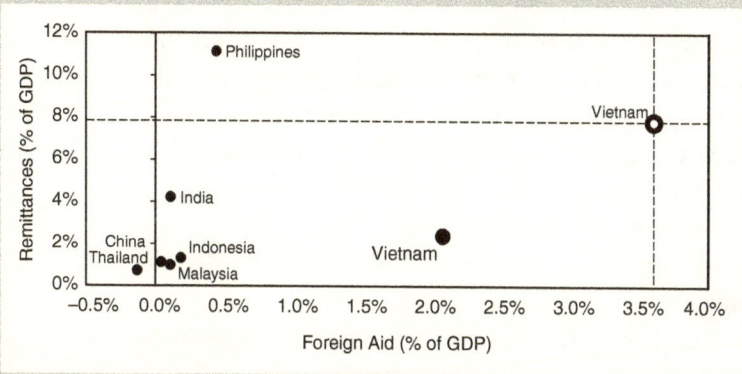

SOURCE: World Bank Development Indicators.

Looking forward to the next three years, Vietnam is expected to continue to enjoy its strategic strengths of location, political stability, and human capital to further deepen its integration into the world economy.

The government is expected to make more strenuous efforts in improving the business environment and to provide more attractive incentives to promote foreign and domestic investment. In these favourable conditions, however, Vietnam will face the following three major challenges, which it needs to address fundamentally to enhance the country's economic performance. The first challenge concerns infrastructure development and environmental protection as the problems of poor urban planning, traffic congestion, and industrial pollution have become severe in the major cities and industrial centres. The second challenge is related to human capital formation and technological capacity building. On various indicators with regard to availability of skilled labour and technological capacity, Vietnam is significantly behind its Asian peers, especially China and Thailand. The third challenge is about the low quality of governance, which has been the root cause of many serious problems, ranging from mismanagement of state assets to macroeconomic instability. The case of Vinashin — the state-owned shipbuilding group — can serve as an illustration. The company has received billions of U.S. dollars from government guaranteed loans to invest in numerous non-viable projects in the government's ambition to turn this state-owned conglomerate into a leading driver of the economy. At the same time, the corporate governance system is weak and corruption is severe. Consequently, in 2010, the chairman and a number of the key members of the company were arrested for mismanagement and dishonest practices. Furthermore, the government had to make major structural interventions to rescue the company from bankruptcy caused by a debt amounting to US$4–5 billion. Weak governance has also been the root cause behind the country's macroeconomic instability.

Relative to its Asian peers, Vietnam has performed poorly on key macroeconomic indicators in recent years, especially during the 2008–09 global financial crisis. The inflation rate was 15 per cent for 2008–09 and 8.6 per cent for 2010 (Figure 5a); while the budget deficit was –7.4 per cent for 2008–09 and –7 per cent for 2010 (Figure 5b). At the same time, the trade deficit as share of GDP was 11.5 per cent for 2008–09 and 11 per cent for 2010, while all its Asian peers, except for the Philippines, ran trade surpluses (Figure 5c). Furthermore, Vietnam's currency relative to the U.S. dollar has been consecutively weakening in both 2008–09 and 2010, while those of its peers are tending to appreciate notably over 2008–10 (Figure 5d). The deterioration in macroeconomic conditions has

Figure 5. Selected Macro Economic Indicators: Vietnam vs. Asian Peers

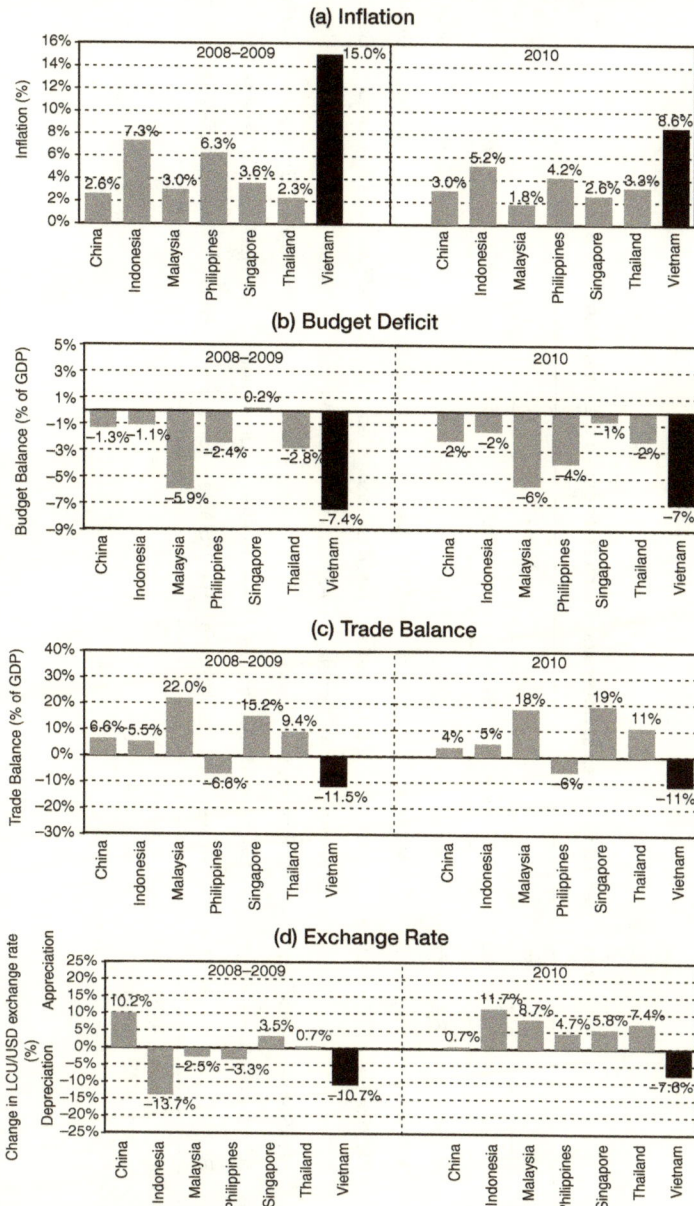

(a) Inflation

(b) Budget Deficit

(c) Trade Balance

(d) Exchange Rate

NOTES: Data for 2010 are estimates.
SOURCE: Author's calculations; data from Economist Intelligence Unit.

Table 1. Recent Changes in Sovereign Credit Ratings: Vietnam vs. Asian Peers

Country	S&P			Moody's			Fitch		
	2008*	2010**	Change	2008*	2010**	Change	2008*	2010**	Change
Vietnam	BB/Stable	BB/Negative	Worse	Ba3/Positive	Ba3/Negative	Worse	BB-/Stable	B+/Stable	Worse
China	A/Positive	A+/Stable	Better	A1/Stable	A1/Stable	Unchanged	A+/Stable	A+/Stable	Unchanged
Indonesia	BB-/Stable	BB/Positive	Better	Ba3/Stable	Ba2/Positive	Better	BB-/Positive	BB+/Stable	Better
Malaysia	A-/Positive	A-/Stable	Worse	A3/Stable	A3/Stable	Unchanged	A-/Stable	A-/Stable	Unchanged
Philippines	BB-/Stable	BB-/Stable	Unchanged	B1/Stable	Ba3/Stable	Better	BB/Stable	BB/Stable	Unchanged
Singapore	AAA/Stable	AAA/Stable	Unchanged	Aaa/Stable	Aaa/Stable	Unchanged	AAA/Stable	AAA/Stable	Unchanged
Thailand	BBB+/Stable	BBB+/Negative	Worse	Baa1/Stable	Baa1/Stable	Unchanged	BBB+/Stable	BBB/Stable	Worse

NOTES: * As at 10 January 2009; ** As at 6 November 2010.
SOURCES: Data from ADB Asia Bond Online <http://asianbondsonline.adb.org/>.

Vietnam: Selected Economic Indicators, 2006–2012F

	2006	2007	2008	2009	2010F	2011F	2012F
GDP growth (% change)	8.2	8.5	6.2	5.3	6.7	7.0	6.9
— Industry sector growth (% change)	10.4	10.2	6.1	5.5	7.5	7.0	8.0
— Services sector growth (% change)	8.3	8.9	7.2	6.6	7.7	8.6	7.4
— Agriculture sector growth (% change)	3.7	3.8	4.1	1.8	3.2	3.0	2.9
Exports (US$ million)	39,826	48,561	62,685	57,096	62,235	70,947	98,056
Imports (US$ million)	42,602	58,921	75,467	65,402	72,073	79,280	–108,330
Trade balance (US$ million)	–2,776	–10,438	–12,782	–8,306	–9,836	–8,330	–10,274
Current account balance (% of GDP)	–0.3	–9.8	–11.8	–7.4	–7.5	–5.4	–6.9
Inflation/CPI average (% change)	7.5	8.3	23.0	6.9	8.5	7.5	7.7
M2 money supply growth (% change)	33.6	46.1	20.3	29.0	19.1	22.0	24.5
Fiscal balance (% of GDP)	–1.2	–5.5	–4.1	–11.8	–7.0	–6.1	–5.7
Total debt outstanding (US$ million)	20,126	23,865	26,158	27,842	33,448	36,557	39,803
Debt service ratio (% of exports)	2.1	2.2	1.9	1.6	1.4	1.5	1.4
Foreign exchange reserves (US$ million)	13,382.5	23,471.8	23,882.0	16,027.4	17,500.0	17,500.0	21,000.0
Exchange rate at year-end (Dong/US$1)	16,054.0	16,114.0	16,977.0	17,941.0	19,495.0	19,950.0	20,351.0

NOTES: E refers to estimates; F refers to forecasts.
SOURCES: Asian Development Bank, World Bank, Economist Intelligence Unit, HSBC.

resulted in the downgrading of Vietnam's sovereign rating recently by all the three major credit rating agencies — S&P, Moody's, and Fitch — while it is worth noting that most of the comparison countries have improved their sovereign rating over the period (Table 1 on page 178). Vietnam's strengths and challenges presented above are the main factors that determine the country's economic outlook over the coming period 2011–12.

THE CONTRIBUTORS

Political Outlook

Ian Baird is Assistant Professor of Geography at the University of Wisconsin, Madison.

Terence Chong is Senior Fellow in the Regional Social and Cultural Studies Programme of the Institute of Southeast Asian Studies.

N. Ganesan is Professor at the Hiroshima Peace Institute. He thanks Lam Peng Er for his comments on an earlier draft of his contribution to this volume.

Douglas Kammen is Assistant Professor in the Southeast Asian Studies Programme of the National University of Singapore.

David Koh is Senior Fellow in the Regional Strategic and Political Studies Programme of the Institute of Southeast Asian Studies.

Maria Ortuoste is Assistant Professor of Political Science at California State University, East Bay, and a former head of the Center of International Relations and Strategic Studies in the Philippines' Foreign Service Institute.

Bernhard Platzdasch is Visiting Research Fellow at the Institute of Southeast Asian Studies.

Rodolfo C. Severino, a former Philippine diplomat and ASEAN Secretary-General, is head of the ASEAN Studies Centre at the Institute of Southeast Asian Studies.

Sokbunthoeun So is a member of the Cambodia Research Group, Faculty of Social Science, VU University Amsterdam (http://www.cambodiaresearch.org).

Ian Storey is Fellow in the Regional Strategic and Political Studies Programme of the Institute of Southeast Asian Studies and editor of the journal *Contemporary Southeast Asia*.

Pushpa Thambipillai teaches in the Faculty of Business, Economics and Policy Studies of the University of Brunei Darussalam.

Tin Maung Maung Than is Senior Fellow in the Regional Strategic and Political Studies Programme of the Institute of Southeast Asian Studies.

Geoff Wade is a historian with an interest in Sino-Southeast Asian interactions. A longer, more detailed version of his contribution to this volume is available at < http://asiapacific.anu.edu.au/newmandala/2010/12/23/asean-divides/ >.

Barry Wain is Writer in Residence at the Institute of Southeast Asian Studies and author of *Malaysian Maverick: Mahathir Mohamad in Turbulent Times*.

Donald E. Weatherbee is Donald S. Russell Distinguished Professor Emeritus at the University of South Carolina.

Matthew Wheeler is a doctoral candidate at the University of New South Wales.

Economic Outlook

Chia Wai Mun is Assistant Professor in the Division of Economics, School of Humanities and Social Sciences at Nanyang Technological University, Singapore.

Sanchita Basu Das is Lead Researcher for Economic Affairs in the ASEAN Studies Centre at the Institute of Southeast Asian Studies.

Francis E. Hutchinson is Visiting Fellow in the Regional Economic Studies Unit at the Institute of Southeast Asian Studies.

Hikari Ishido is Visiting Fellow in the Regional Economic Studies Unit at the Institute of Southeast Asian Studies, and Associate Professor, Faculty of Law and Economics, Chiba University, Japan.

Kian-Teng Kwek is Associate Professor in the Department of Economics, Faculty of Economics and Administration, at Malaya University, Malaysia.

Li Mengling is a doctoral candidate in the Division of Economics, School of Humanities and Social Sciences at Nanyang Technological University, Singapore.

Jayant Menon is Principal Economist in the Office for Regional Economic Integration at the Asian Development Bank, Manila, the Philippines.

Sakulrat Montreevat is Senior Assistant Director at the Economics and Finance Institute, Bangkok, Thailand.

Kyophilavong Phouphet is Associate Professor in the Faculty of Economics and Business Management at the National University of Laos, Vientiane, Laos.

Aladdin D. Rillo is International Consultant (Macroeconomist) at the Asian Development Bank, Manila, the Philippines.

Reza Siregar is Director of Research and Learning Content at the South East Asian Central Banks (SEACEN) Research and Training Centre in Kuala Lumpur, Malaysia.

Sng Hui Ying is Research Associate in the Division of Economics, School of Humanities and Social Sciences at Nanyang Technological University, Singapore.

Thein Swe is Lecturer, Economics and International Finance, International Business MBA Program in the Faculty of Business Administration, and South East Asian Institute of Global Studies at Payap University, Chiang Mai, Thailand.

Moe Thuzar is Lead Researcher for Socio-cultural Affairs in the ASEAN Studies Centre at the Institute of Southeast Asian Studies.

Vu Minh Khuong is Assistant Professor in the Lee Kuan Yew School of Public Policy at the National University of Singapore, Singapore.

THE EDITORS

Michael J. Montesano is Visiting Research Fellow at the Institute of Southeast Asian Studies.

Lee Poh Onn is Fellow and Joint Coordinator in the Regional Economic Studies Unit at the Institute of Southeast Asian Studies.